ENDORSEMENTS

Wow! What a timely book for these times we are all living in! In this book you're holding, Joseph Z has included keys to understanding the times and flourishing in them!

This is not another Jezebel book, but every church leader and Christian needs to understand the battle we are all in with Jezebel. This spirit has risen more in the past few months than ever before. You and I need to understand this spirit and deal with it permanently, and this book paves the way for that.

We cannot only have the "Issachar anointing" to understand the times. We must also be empowered to roar like lions and defeat the enemy attempting to overtake our family, community, churches, and nation.

Get out your pen and highlighter. Let the Holy Spirit speak to you as you read, and then write your notes in this book! It's time to embrace God's unlimited power and break the Antichrist spirit!

Gene Bailey
Author and Host of *Flashpoint*

The Greater Golden Global Glory Outpouring will restore the Issachar Mantle. This mantle will equip you to know who, what, where, when, and how to act and react during the greatest outpouring of God's Spirit in history!

Sid Israel Roth
Host, *It's Supernatural*

T0356190

Joseph Z is at the forefront of a bold new generation of prophetic voices that God is raising up for such a time as this. *The Spirit of Elijah* reveals how followers of Jesus can step into their God-given destinies by following the timeless example of one of the greatest and most anointed prophets of all: Elijah. With evil and apostasy once again on the rise, much like in Elijah's day, *The Spirit of Elijah* is an absolute must-read for every believer who wants to understand how to thrive and lead in the unprecedented, prophetic times we live in today.

Erick Stakelbeck
Host of TBN's *Stakelbeck Tonight*
and *The Watchman Newscast*

Since the fall of man, there has been a battle between the kingdom of God and the kingdoms of darkness, and throughout history, we can see how it affects nations, cities, and cultures. Yet, the Lord arises in victory to combat the evil agenda of the wicked through an anointing that counters, confronts, and engages; it is with the spirit of Elijah! So much so that when John the Baptist came on the scene, and even when Jesus did, many thought they were, in fact, Elijah himself. This spirit of Elijah must rise in these days, as the scripture foretells, to gather the fathers to the children lest the earth be smitten with a curse. This is why the latest book written by Joseph Z, *The Spirit of Elijah*, is not only a must-read, but it carries that anointing to raise reformers who will stop the onslaught of the wicked. Joseph carries this anointing himself, and as a prophetic reformer, he has imparted it into the very pages of this book, which is truly a war manual for resetting, restoring, and bringing the greatest renewal into modern history.

Pastor Hank Kunneman
Lord of Hosts Church and One Voice Ministries
Omaha, Nebraska

In *The Spirit of Elijah*, Joseph Z delivers a prophetic and timely message about the role of reformers in every generation who are called to confront the darkness and bring restoration. Drawing from biblical examples like Elijah, the Maccabees, and others who stood boldly against the spirit of Antichrist in their day, this book provides a blueprint for how believers can operate in the spirit of Elijah to turn hearts back to God and prepare the way for revival. Joseph Z expertly weaves historical insights, biblical wisdom, and practical application to show how the spirit of reformation that operated through Elijah is still active today, empowering the Church to push back against cultural darkness and reconcile generations. This is an essential read for anyone seeking to understand their role in bringing godly reformation and preparing the way for Christ's return.

Mike Signorelli
Lead Pastor, V1 Church

Joseph Z has delivered a prophetic call to action for our time. The Spirit of Elijah is not just a book, it's a battle plan for reformers in this critical hour. With biblical depth and prophetic clarity, Joseph unveils the ancient spirits that have warred against God's people through the ages and shows us how to stand firm in the power of the spirit of Elijah. He masterfully connects the dots between the challenges of Elijah's time, the spiritual warfare we face today, and the urgent need for generational reconciliation and bold reformers. This book will awaken, equip, and inspire you to confront the darkness, restore hope, and take your place in God's redemptive plan for this generation and beyond.

If you are ready to stand against the Babylonian system, push back the spirit of Antichrist, and become part of God's unstoppable remnant, *The Spirit of Elijah* is a must-read. Prepare to rise as a reformer!

Pastor Todd Coconato
President, Religious Liberties Coalition
Founder, Remnant News, Dallas, Texas

While the Church is crying out, "Where is the Lord God of Elijah?" a voice can be heard from heaven asking, "Where are the Elijahs of God?!" In *The Spirit of Elijah*, Joseph Z accurately diagnoses the times we're living in as a generation overrun by Jezebel's witchcraft and Ahab's compromise. Still, he also equips the reader to rise and cast that spirit down. This isn't a polite book; it's a clarion call to reformers who will refuse to bow to the Babylonian system and instead declare, "If God be God, follow Him!" Joseph weaves together history, prophecy, and practical insight with one goal: to raise up a people who are both discerning like the sons of Issachar and unrelenting like the Maccabees.

I haven't read a book in a long time that has ignited the fire of God within me like this one. If you've ever felt like one voice can't make a difference, this book will shake you out of your slumber. One reformer, filled with the fire of God, can shift a nation. Read it, share it, and then get to work. The reformers are rising. Are you ready to be one of them?

Alan DiDio
Pastor, The Encounter Charlotte
Host of *Encounter Today*

Joseph Z has written a book for today, instructing you and me to be an Elijah, a reformer, to stand up against the evils found in our generation as it was in the days of Ahab and Jezebel. If you are like me, I sometimes feel inadequate to take on that responsibility. But in his epistle, James tells us, "Elijah was a man with a nature like ours" (James 5:17). In other words, if God could use Elijah, He can use you and me. Great book, Joseph. I loved it. You are loosing a new generation of reformers into the earth to usher in the coming of Jesus.

Pastor Bob Yandian
Teacher, Author
Bobyandian.com

We have come to a critical crossroads in history where the darkness is getting darker while the light is growing brighter (Isaiah 60:1-3). In his new book, Joseph Z, a good friend and a prophet in our apostolic network, imparts a timely message for this generation. The time has come for reformers to arise and respond to the call of Daniel 11:32—"But the people who know their God will be strong and take action!" Take this book to heart and partner with the divine assignment on your life!

Dr. Ché Ahn
Senior Leader, Harvest Rock Church, Pasadena, CA
President, Harvest International Ministry
International Chancellor, Wagner University

In an age of unprecedented deception, millions are being swept away by the lies and schemes of the enemy. This is not just a social agenda by the powerful elite, it is also a strategic attack of the spirit of the Antichrist. Joseph Z articulates the Church's next steps in this profound prophetic manual with bold truth and prophetic accuracy. In *Spirit of Elijah*, you will learn how to recognize the sway of the spirit of this age and resist the pool of the great deception that has come upon the earth. Learn biblical strategies to walk in victory in these end times. This is not just a book. It's a secret weapon that exposes the playbook of the enemy.

Dr. Kynan Bridges, President
Kynan Bridges Ministries, Inc.

So many believers today are throwing up their hands in dismay and fretting, "What is going on in this world? Why does it seem that darkness is so often winning?" Joseph Z's work, *The Spirit of Elijah*, is a powerful reminder that the gospel has not lost its effect and that light will win. This book is not just a call to hope, it is a practical road map on how to live in a way that transforms the culture of this age. It's time for the Church to speak up and call forth the fire of reformation.

David Diga Hernandez
Evangelist

I was only a few pages in and felt such a powerful anointing on this book. Frankly, I needed this five years ago! When the evil agenda to hurt our children came full force in 2020, a fire rose inside of me to expose evil and come against it. But as a mom of five kids with no experience in "fighting back," it was a bit awkward because I didn't understand what you will learn in this powerful book! *The Spirit of Elijah* will help you confidently take your position as a modern-day reformer for the glory of God! This is no small thing! You are needed for this great turnaround in our nation!

Jenny Donnelly
Her Voice Movement, Founder
#DontMessWithOurKidsUSA

Prophets do not simply predict future events, they partner with the Holy Spirit to help usher in God's-ordained future. In addition, true prophets equip all believers to hear God for themselves, discern spiritual matters, and cancel the enemy's attempts to interfere with God's "on earth as it is in heaven" agenda. I'm constantly awed that our God is so sovereign that He has factored prophecy and the participation of His people into the unfolding of His plans and purposes on earth. But again, there is a conflict. There is a battle. The age-old principalities and powers that the prophet Elijah challenged among the Baal worshipers of antiquity are very much alive today. They are actively opposing the advancement of God's kingdom. Good news: God has a plan, and this powerful new book is a prophetic blueprint to help you successfully navigate the coming days. This right-on-time word from Joseph Z unpacking the *Spirit of Elijah* will sharpen your ability to hear God's voice, help you discern the times and seasons we live in, and empower you to take your place on the victorious front lines of God's end-time army.

Larry Sparks, MDiv
LM Sparks Ministries, Co-founder and President
Author of *Pentecostal Fire* and *Ask for the Rain*

In a world where the truth and true gospel are rarely taught without apology, Joseph Z is one of the few faith leaders I have met who teaches the gospel without apology. Second Timothy 4:3-4 (KJV) tells us, "The time will come when they will not endure sound doctrine, but after their own lusts shall they heap to themselves teachers, having itching ears; and they shall turn away their ears from the truth, and shall be turned unto fables." Joseph Z's podcasts, sermons, and writings are urgently needed in a world that has begun to heap itself to teachers preaching fables instead of the irrefutable Word of God known as the Bible.

Clay Clark
Father of five kids
Host of the 6X iTunes chart-topping *ThrivetimeShow.com* podcast
Former SBA Entrepreneur of the Year
Amazon best-selling author
Founder of several multimillion dollar businesses

I am truly honored to endorse *The Spirit of Elijah*. Prophet Z has proven to be an accurate prophetic voice and has been a blessing to me and my family. His understanding of the current times is remarkable, and his teachings have strengthened the body of Christ.

This book is a profound resource for anyone seeking to receive and embrace the Spirit of Elijah. In the days ahead, Jezebel will try to pollute the land, but God will raise up His Elijahs. May the words of this book be like a fresh fire from heaven in your hands!

Pastor Brian Gibson
Gibsonministries.com

My friend Joseph Z has written more than a book. This is a prophetic declaration of immense importance. He is challenging the prophetic movement to arise to new levels of function. This is necessary if we are to see the Church release its voice and culture be shifted. Bravo, my friend!

Robert Henderson
https://www.roberthendersonministries.com/

Joseph Z's book *The Spirit of Elijah* is a must-read if you want to be equipped to discern the times and seasons of God for the hour. This book has a blueprint to know God more and overcome the present-day powers of darkness. You will be amazed as Joseph releases a fresh and victorious approach to overcoming warfare in your life. You will be empowered to walk closer to God's heart. Read and be equipped for victory, and understand what God is doing and will do in this next season. A generation is being set apart for great exploits, and *The Spirit of Elijah* prepares you to join this company of overcomers who will overthrow the devil's plans and make Jesus famous on earth today. Enjoy!

Jerame Nelson
Elisha Revolution
Author, *Burning Ones: Calling Forth a Generation of Dread Champions* and *Encountering Angels*

In a world where darkness is desperate to write the prevailing narrative, we see a divine solution come forth. In moments of crisis and conflict, the reformers arise, those with confidence and boldness in their God that defies all opinions, commentaries, and chatter surrounding them. I believe we are truly living in an hour when the spirit of Elijah is becoming more apparent by the day. Who will be the sons and daughters of God who confront the kingdom of darkness with one simple question: If the god you serve is the Lord, let him speak, but if the God I serve is the Lord, may every enemy be scattered!

Ross Johnston
Revivalist
Rossjohnston.co/

Years ago, I had an encounter with the Lord where He invited me to believe for more than revival. "Revival in the churches unto reformation in the nations" is what He told me He desired. I have never forgotten that. Of course, we need revival. We need souls saved. We need bodies healed. We need people delivered. But we also, just as much, need nations and spheres of influence impacted and changed. We need revival in our churches…unto reformation in our nations. This new book from Joseph Z—*The Spirit of Elijah*—will help enlighten, equip, and empower a generation of reformers who will heal and deliver nations as much as all the wonderful revivalists will heal and deliver souls. Thank you, Joseph, for the wisdom and insights of this book and the spiritual substance and impartation you poured into *The Spirit of Elijah*. May every person who reads it be set ablaze with the fire of God's counsel and might, and may they be part of this next generation of reformers who really and truly change the world!

Robert Hotchkin
Founder, Robert Hotchkin Ministries and Men on the Frontlines
Host, *The Truth About Men* TV show
roberthotchkin.com

This book will encourage current and future generations to live and walk in God's calling on their lives and stand mightily against the forces of darkness under the anointing of the Spirit. It will challenge readers to jump off the fence and begin battling evil with the same ferocity as Elijah. Joseph writes in a way that is easy to understand yet carries with it the weight of real truth, as he does not shy away from telling it like it is.

Troy Black
Christian YouTuber, Author, Prophetic Voice
troyblackvideos.com

As I read, I was deeply moved by the message of hope that even in the face of unyielding darkness, God has equipped His people to stand, discern the times, and carry His mandate forward. The call to be a reformer is not reserved for prophets on mountaintops; it is for every believer who desires to see God's will prevail in their families, communities, and nations.

In *The Spirit of Elijah*, Joseph Z reminds us that we are part of a larger, multigenerational narrative. This book is a must-read for anyone longing to walk boldly in their calling during these critical times. The truths in these pages will inspire you to rise, take your place, and make a difference for future generations.

Don't just read this book—let its message ignite a fire in you to confront the darkness and be a light in this generation. It couldn't be timelier, and it's a resource the body of Christ desperately needs.

Mondo De La Vega
Host of *The Mondo*
Co-host of the *Jim Bakker Show*
Author of *My Crazy Life:*
The Moments That Brought a Gangster to Grace
themondoshow.com

In *The Spirit of Elijah*, Joseph Z delivers a prophetic exploration of our times, exposing the rise of the Antichrist spirit and unveiling the reforming power of Elijah to confront evil, reconcile generations, and break corruption. With vivid biblical insights, Joseph Z provides a prophetic road map for the last days, challenging readers to discern the times, push back the darkness, and rise as "beast-proof" reformers. It is a must-read for those ready to fulfill their purpose in God's plan.

Steve Ram
Business Owner, Investor, Independent Journalist
www.SteveRamNews.com

The Spirit of Elijah is a manifesto for warrior reformers everywhere. A call to spiritual arms and a summons to the frontlines of modern history. This book puts into words what many sense in the Spirit. However, I must warn you that this book should come with a warning. If read through completely, with a desperate heart, you will have an encounter with God that will forever change your destiny. Joseph Z is part of my chosen family and is a friend who provokes me to love Jesus more. He is a rare prophet of purity and power. He writes with the spirit of prophecy upon him.

Dr. Malachi A. O'Brien
Malachi Media Group

So many people are battling discouragement today as they witness a tide of unprecedented evil rising globally. It appears that darkness has gained the upper hand. But there is good news for believers who are determined to endure! The Lord has been and is mightily at work preparing His people for the ultimate confrontation between the forces of darkness and the Kingdom of Light.

In his new book, *The Spirit of Elijah*, Joseph Z brilliantly highlights that we are on the brink of one of the greatest seasons of victory the body of Christ has ever been entrusted with and provides valuable insights on what we can do to be part of God's masterful plan. From the familiar Old Testament account of Elijah confronting the spirits of Jezebel and Ahab, Joseph reveals powerful truths that will not only encourage you but will empower and position you to tear down every evil stronghold.

Mark Cowart
Senior Pastor, Church For All Nations
Colorado Springs, Colorado

The Spirit of Elijah is an end-time prophetic promise that awakens a new generation of reformers to turn the nation back to God. The last days will be marked by an end-time prophetic generation that will walk in the spirit and power of Elijah. Like Elijah, these reformers will speak the truth, and bring repentance and reformation that will transform nations. This groundbreaking book by Joseph Z will awaken you to a place of deep hunger and provide you with the clarity you need to walk in this end-time prophetic promise. Now is your time!

Dr. Charles Karuku
Lead Pastor, The Hub
Burnsville, Minnesota

Joseph Z is more than a prophetic voice to our generation—he carries the mantle of a spiritual father, inspiring and equipping God's remnant to fulfill their divine calling in these pivotal times. Whether through his meetings, videos, or books, Joseph's relentless passion for empowering believers to walk boldly in their God-given purpose is unmistakable.

In *The Spirit of Elijah*, Joseph does more than teach the mission of the Elijah Generation—he sets it in motion. With clarity and conviction, he challenges believers to rise, confront the forces of Ahab and

Jezebel, dismantle Baal's strongholds, and courageously and authoritatively reject Babylon's influence.

This is not just a book—it's a prophetic charge, a rallying cry, and a road map for revival. Scripture declares that the spirit of Elijah will turn hearts, reconcile generations, and prepare the way for God's kingdom. Joseph masterfully connects this timeless promise to today's pressing challenges, offering practical tools to help believers reclaim their divine purpose and advance the kingdom with power.

The Spirit of Elijah is more than a message—it's a movement and a call to action for those ready to see transformation in their lives and their generation. This book is your guide if you're prepared to embrace your destiny and be part of a supernatural shift. Don't just read it—live it!

Larry Ragland
Pastor, Solid Rock, Birmingham, Alabama
Host, *The Big Picture* TV and Online Show
Founder, Ambassadors Network & College
Author, *I See Greatness In You* and other books

Joseph Z delivers a prophetic and timely message for the hour we are living in. He exposes the Antichrist spirit at work in the world and reveals how God is raising a generation of reformers who will not bow to Baal. They are coming in the spirit and power of Elijah, anointed and unshakable, ready to push back against the enemy's agenda!

This book is a clarion call to action. As you read, you'll feel a holy fire stir within you to rise in the authority of Christ and boldly declare, "Not on my watch!" Don't miss this urgent word—let it awaken something deep inside you and propel you into the fight for righteousness!

Matt Cruz
Evangelist
MattCruz.com

This book is a must for anyone serious about the prophetic, this move of God, and the supernatural. It is based on the written Word of God and is easy to understand! I wanted to underline almost every word and could hardly put it down. I felt like I was in Bible school, learning and being taught new and fresh revelation. *The Spirit of Elijah* book will help expedite this brand-new move of the supernatural with a solid foundation that can reveal "how" to walk with the Lord in this dimension.

Joseph Z is a noted, sound, and proven prophet. His dedication and devotion to the Lord and his calling are very inspiring. He's surrounded by ministers who have walked closely with the Lord and have a proven ministry, which is crucial for him to advance deeper as a prophet of God with a true "thus saith it" in his mouth. Joseph and his whole family are in this together, making for a firm platform to minister to the Lord's precious people. His gift of seeing is amazing, as is Joseph's revelation of what he sees and how to use it properly for today's situations!

I highly recommend this book, not just to read but to study carefully and receive from the anointing that is on his life and in the words of this book! Get ready to learn how to go higher and higher into those realms of the spirit!

Ginger Ziegler
Ginger Ziegler Ministries

Besides being a close friend and one of the most powerful and accurate prophets of our time, Joseph Z is an excellent teacher. This book is full of deep revelations for those who want to understand more of the spiritual world and the things that seem mystical or hard to understand. Joseph uses his incredibly strong, revelatory gift to prophesy and teach these deep, spiritual truths that God has revealed to him. When I was 18, I wrote a song called "Where are the Elijahs?" This book is a clarion call for that same question. This book will help the Elijahs of today to rise and remember that the God who answers by fire remains the same and is still backing up the Elijahs of our age with mighty power, signs, and wonders.

Ben Diaz, Senior Pastor
Vida Church, Mesa, Arizona
Author, *Radical Healing*
vidachurchaz.com @pastorbendiaz

The Spirit of Elijah is the missing element in the Church today and the anointing that guarantees her victory. Good News! God is pouring out the spirit of Elijah on the Church in these last days. Joseph Z brings this prophetic, end-times scripture smack into our present world, where the spirit of the age is making its final assault. Let's go, Church. It's game on.

Pastor Ken Peters
Senior Pastor, Patriot Church

In our times, with constant challenges, Joseph Z provides a timely message for every season. *The Spirit of Elijah* is an essential resource to empower the reformer within you to stand firm against the evils of our age. I have been a lifelong friend of Joseph, and I feel honored to know a man of God like him. Thank you for writing this necessary book for our generation and those to come.

Joshua Ercoli
Founder, Souled Out International

When he stood ready to call down fire from heaven in the face of the hundreds of enemy prophets, Elijah, the reformer, was all alone going into battle for the true God. That same spirit of Elijah is rising today, and an army of reformers needs to be ready for what's coming. Joseph Z's prophetic understanding of scripture and insight into today's world is accurate and trustworthy. His clear revelation and teaching will unlock supernatural results and equip you to stand against the Antichrist system, which rises in opposition to the true God.

John Matarazzo
Charisma News

The Spirit of Elijah is a must-have! If you loved *Breaking Hell's Economy* and *Servants of Fire*, then *The Spirit of Elijah* is for you. This is a *Now Word* and a prophetic book on what is to come! Joseph Z has been on point with so many revelations in this last season when many prophets have missed it. *The Spirit of Elijah* will walk you through many questions you might have had about what's about to happen in this crazy world. If you are interested in not what happened but what's coming ahead, *The Spirit of Elijah* is for you! To be pre-warned is to be forearmed!

Ryan Edberg
Founder, Kingdom Youth Conference

THE SPIRIT OF
ELIJAH

Harrison
House

Shippensburg, PA

Harrison House Books by Joseph Z

*Demystifying the Prophetic: Understanding the
Voice of God for the Coming Days of Fire*

*Servants of Fire: Secrets of the Unseen War &
Angels Fighting for You*

*Breaking Hell's Economy: Your Guide to
Last-Days Supernatural Provision*

Breaking Hell's Economy Study Manual

Jesus and the Kingmakers

The Origin of the Cosmic Battle

*The Spirit of Elijah: Expose the Truth. Embrace
God's Power. Break the Antichrist Spirit.*

*The Secret to the Life of John: A Revelation for
a Supernaturally Long-Lasting Life*

Weaponizing Your Faith

JOSEPH Z

THE SPIRIT OF
ELIJAH

EXPOSE THE TRUTH.
EMBRACE GOD'S POWER.
BREAK THE ANTICHRIST SPIRIT.

Published by Harrison House Publishers

Shippensburg, PA 17257

ISBN 13 TP: 978-1-6675-0608-1

ISBN 13 eBook: 978-1-6675-0609-8

For Worldwide Distribution, Printed in the U.S.A.

1 2025

DEDICATION

Due to the nature of what this message represents, I wish to dedicate this book to my children and grandchildren—Alison, Jeremy, her husband, and indeed my son Daniel. I dedicate this book to all of you and our newest addition—our granddaughter. She is joining us near the release of this book, and we are thrilled to welcome her! This book is for all the generations that will follow you in our family line.

Psalm 102:18 reads, "This will be written for the generation to come, that a people yet to be created may praise the LORD."

I pray that my children's children and beyond will read this book. What I wrote is for them, as a generation to come, those who are yet to be created, that they will arrive and praise the Lord!

To you, my children, and future generations. I love you; I believe in you—live for Jesus, and you will impact the world for eternity. We will all meet here or on the other side of the veil, and I anticipate that surreal and glorious day.

ACKNOWLEDGMENTS

Each book I write is a unique project with a special message and a life of its own. When a book project is completed, the presence of those who worked alongside me during its conception and completion enhances it.

Without each of the tremendous people I am surrounded by, the message of a book like this would not reach its highest destination. Therefore, let me mention some people who helped make this book possible.

First and always, my amazing wife, Heather, followed by my two adult children, Alison and her husband Jeremy, and our amazing son, Daniel. You are my best friends. Thank you for your constant support while writing this book and the many daily projects you assisted me with. I love each one of you.

Rick Renner, I don't think you will ever realize how much you mean to me and the inspiration you have been in my life to write and do ministry to the very highest and best unto the Lord. You consistently challenge me to be better in every way. My life has been tremendously impacted by who you are and your obedience to Jesus. I honor you and am most grateful that we can walk together and serve Jesus.

Mary Ercoli, your dedication and hard work inspire me to do better and rise higher constantly. Thank you for your diligence and belief in this project. Your discipline and commitment are astonishing! I am honored to work with you.

Every day during this process, several people make everything work.

Jason Chandler, thank you for all your support and care and for traveling with us for many years. You are not only a friend but have played a vital role in helping us impact lives worldwide. Many years ago, you went from harvesting crops across the nation to assisting us in harvesting souls and making disciples. When I started this book, our nearly non-stop travel had us home only five days out of every month, and you have gone with us on each trip. I often looked up from writing to communicate with you as we arrived at our next meeting. Your commitment to helping organize so much of our work means more to us and this ministry than we could ever fully convey. Thank you, sir!

Holly Eide, how you oversee the scope and ether of our many workers abroad is a high skill! Thank you for your time and efforts. From the day you joined us, we have seen growth and monumental advancements. What you bring daily to this ministry and all its wonderful people is amazing. You are a gift!

Arielle Carver, what can I say? You keep me on track every day. Thank you for your discernment and for being part of this ministry for many years! You carry a gift of wisdom and a refreshing organizational structure that gets actual results. You and Brandon have made a major impact on our lives. Thank you for saying yes.

Elijah Bulgin, there are not enough words to describe how much value you bring daily. Your work ethic is so far above and beyond, and you do the daily work of an entire media department. Thank you for traveling the world with me these past few years and creating daily programs for our viewers. Good things come from Russia! It is an honor to have such a dedicated man of God as part of this assignment. I believe in you and can only thank you for dedicating yourself to becoming who God has called you to be and standing with me to build content and get the message out to so many daily. Thank you, E.

To all my staff and team, thank you for being amazing people and believers. Thank you for representing Jesus to our partners, followers, and friends through this ministry. I have the greatest staff and team in the world!

Our partners…you mean the world to us. We pray daily and thank God for you. Our constant prayer is to gain wisdom and discernment about how to pray for you and see the Lord's blessing manifest in your life. Thank you for your faithfulness and support. We love you!

CONTENTS

FOREWORDS

The book of Malachi indicates that Elijah, the prophet, will return before the Great and Terrible Day of the Lord. In this timely book, Joseph Z has laid out with great clarity how the conflict between the spirit of the age and the need for the Elijah anointing to emerge in the body of Christ. You are going to receive special, deep understanding and an astonishing revelation as you read and digest within your spirit the powerful insight the Holy Spirit has given him. Joseph is an anointed minister for this generation and a prophetic voice for our time. It is important that when God speaks through vessels such as Joseph, we pay careful attention as it will be a prophetic word in season.

Perry Stone
Founder and Director
Voice of Evangelism

Whew...what a book!

This book took me off guard because it *far* surpassed my expectations. Because it came from my dear friend Joseph Z's heart, mind, and hands, I expected it to be good, but the breadth and depth of this book truly *amazed* me. I have long had the highest regard for Joseph, but what is articulated in these pages far surpasses anything I've seen that he has written. With each new chapter, I found myself *stunned* at the genius manner in which the Holy Spirit enabled Joseph to package the truth about a culture gone mad with history, politics, revelation, and how God's people are to respond prophetically.

The name of this book is *The Spirit of Elijah*—and by using the example of the prophet Elijah, Joseph makes a convincing case that it is time for "the spirit of Elijah" to move mightily in the Church in these last days. Indeed, God is calling on the Church to—like Elijah and others like him—stand up for truth and righteousness, confront a culture gone mad, and hasten the coming of the Lord!

Those who are spiritually aware know that many nations around the world are in the clutches of dark forces that are waging a conflict against godliness. This deceptive war lulls those affected by its spell into an unconcerned state, even as the world sinks slowly into the dark mire of depravity. Joseph says, in effect, "Even now, the war is here—it is confronting you. We see darkness continually rising, but God would never allow society to operate under the complete dominance of evil without offering weapons and mechanisms to respond and fight back. The great God of heaven has a secret weapon available to you." And truth be told, as Joseph communicates in this book, God's first and last line of defense *and* offense in this world is YOU! He has given you divine power that is crucial to countering the culture of the times.

Again and again, in this book, my friend Joseph writes about *reformers*—those whom God has called to step forward as agents of clarity to speak uncompromising truth to bring an adjustment to a generation that has gone astray. Joseph shows from the Bible and history that in each generation, God has called reformers to stand and to use their authority—and that in this time, when nations around the world are in the *clutches* of dark forces, God is once again calling for such men and women to heed His call and step forward to be His voice of clarity and light in a confused world.

Joseph skillfully draws on the example of Elijah as a reformer. Elijah not only possessed revelation, but he also moved in the power of God.

Joseph writes that true God-called reformers, like Elijah, show up with a revelation and the power of God needed to confront the culture of our day. He states that this Holy Spirit horsepower is a dinner bell to the world and the method by which God shakes the complacent and gives evil cause to pause. Oh how today's Church needs reformers with revelation and divine power to back it up!

Unfortunately, there are legitimate prophets who know what God wants to say, but because they have been intimidated by the spirit of the age, they have been stopped from speaking out on various issues that God wants to address in this generation. Add to this a widespread apostasy that is creeping into the mainstream, and now—more than ever—it's time for God's end-time reformers and His prophetic voices to arise and answer the wickedness *in the spirit of Elijah!*

Not only is this the task of well-known prophetic voices and recognized reformers, but it is also the task of *every believer* to be a light, to stand up without fear, and to do as Elijah did in his generation. For this reason, I assure you that this book is a must-read for *everyone*, not just for prophets and established reformers.

Joseph says, "You were born for the days we are in right now. It doesn't matter your age or station in life. All that matters is answering the high call of the great God of heaven. Your *yes* is all He needs. Keep giving it to Him, and you will see the goodness of the Lord in the land of the living. A generational clarion call has come and is awaiting your answer. It is a mass calling to prophetic voices and God's people at large to embrace the anointing of reformers and to rise in the spirit of Elijah!"

In my experience with Joseph's ministry over the years, I often hear him say, "EVEN ON A BAD DAY, YOU ARE ANOINTED TO BE THE BEST THERE IS!" Indeed, you must never forget that you are called, chosen, and anointed for this hour. It is time for *you*—and everyone who has an ear to hear what the Spirit is saying—to step forward as God's prophetic voice to confront and bring deliverance to an erring end-time generation in need of God's redemptive power!

Honestly, I cannot give a higher recommendation than I am giving for this book. Please don't make the mistake of purchasing it and then letting it sit unread on a coffee table or shelf. You need to devour this book and take its content deeply into your spirit and mind. Both God and a lost world are waiting for YOU to hear the call of God to step forward in *the spirit of Elijah!*

Rick Renner, ThD
Minister, Author, Broadcaster
Moscow, Russia

INTRODUCTION

This book resulted from my desire to understand what the prophet Malachi meant when he prophetically declared, "I will send you Elijah the prophet before the coming of the great and dreadful day of the Lord." My discoveries in scripture led me to write this book as both a prophetic briefing for each generation and a call to action against the nefarious powers that would try to subject our children to their wicked agendas.

> Behold, I will send you Elijah the prophet before the coming of the great and dreadful day of the LORD. [6] And he will turn the hearts of the fathers to the children, and the hearts of the children to their fathers, lest I come and strike the earth with a curse.
>
> —Malachi 4:5-6

Vital to me was understanding the how-to of Elijah's assignment. How would he turn the hearts of the fathers back to the children and vice versa? What would that look like?

I wanted to understand Malachi's prophecy, as well as the nature of the spirit of Elijah in our generation. After all, the agency of Elijah being sent orchestrates and executes generational restoration, an absolute necessity to avoid the curse.

For projects like this one, a mistake can be made in an attempt to navigate or define Elijah's prophetic mission based on opinion, not scripture. A solid biblical foundation was a must for me when look-ing at the prophetic word Malachi spoke regarding Elijah's coming. In addition, I desire to avoid label-casting a catchy term, and further, to avoid the term "Spirit of Elijah" from becoming mis-defined. Avoiding the adage, "Metaphors reign where mysteries reside," meaning, often when individuals don't fully grasp a topic or issue, they give it some metaphorical, or even allegorical *typecast* definition, which, again, does not portray the Lord's intent.

Tragically, mis-defined truths can stumble or overly spiritualize their way into a nebulous, poorly conceived pseudo-Christian lingo dictionary. Our current spiritual pop culture is filled with many popu-larized ideas; but without scriptural due diligence, the true significance of the message could be missed. However, with a strong scriptural foundation, the message will go from capsizing to rightsizing, offering legitimate results to the reader.

In the case of *The Spirit of Elijah*, it was of the highest importance to me that you, the reader, could grasp and clearly understand the mes-sage and theme while attaining a sense of empowerment to act.

My purpose in writing this was to convey that no matter what we face in our generation, many have experienced the same things before us. I hope this book offers informative clarity and boldness to act in the face of an Antichrist spirit—opposing all evil that seeks to bind the uninformed and drive the culture into a moral void and demonic slavery. I trust that the lights of revelatory understanding will ignite as you read this book, and I pray that the Bible will come alive with clarity on this vital issue. May this be a beginning point for you to play a part in transforming our current generation.

A man or woman with a revelation from God is not at the mercy of a culture going mad. Instead, they will discover righteous authority, which transcends what the Western world has taught us about doing church. A revelation of God's will based on His Word and the patterns we see throughout scripture is paramount when dealing with generational travesty. This book is for Elijah; this book is for every person who has stood up against the mechanisms of an Antichrist spirit—this book is for you.

The spirit of Elijah is defined as standing against the oppression of an evil regime while operating in generational cooperation. This narrative of generational cooperation is not limited to a single era. Still, it spans across generations, seeing the will of God and His people come to pass in a multigenerational capacity. It's a larger, enduring narrative that we, as believers, are part of.

When we consider all the scripture references regarding the spirit of Elijah, it becomes clear that this term, often used in pop culture Christianity, has a deeper significance. My purpose for using the phrase "spirit of Elijah" is to define the familiar conflict of national and even global powers that seek to usurp the authority given by God for the good of humanity. It's about activating those who would rise with a word from God to oppose such forces.

As a prophet, Elijah was tasked with enforcing God's will in his generation and passing on a generational anointing. This act of empowerment, symbolized by the transfer of his mantle to Elisha, ensured that the spirit of Elijah would continue to influence and guide future generations.

Today, the spirit of Elijah is available to the Church of Jesus Christ to prepare the way once again for His return. You, dear reader, are invited to be part of changing the world!

Joseph Z

CHAPTER ONE

ONE REFORMER
VERSUS AN ARMY
OF DARKNESS

*Now therefore send, and gather to me all Israel unto
mount Carmel, and the prophets of Baal four hundred
and fifty, and the prophets of the groves four hundred,
which eat at Jezebel's table.*

—1 Kings 18:19 KJV

Prophets of darkness stood in assembly—*450 prophets of Baal,
with 400 prophets of the female goddess Asherah* who dined at
the vile table of Jezebel. Together, they awaited the arrival of
the one King Ahab labeled the "troubler of Israel." These prophets and
all of Israel came together at the prophet's request. The same prophet
who declared no rain would come to their land. A gathering of this
kind would not have occurred had the nation not suffered drought and
famine. These idolatrous figures, with their king among them, would
not have answered such a roll call unless the circumstances were so
dire. On this day, however, all in attendance stood in anticipation of
the arrival of the prophet Elijah.

God's strategy is remarkable when you consider this situation. Not
unlike Samson's final act, where the Lord orchestrated the demise of
those wicked elites who were celebrating, that is, until Samson found

his place between the two central columns of the building. In his death, he destroyed more evildoers than in his entire life (Judges 16:30). The Lord may use circumstances like this to correct or rightsize a nation. In one moment, through years of preparation, even by great difficulty, the stage is set, the pieces are in place, the right players are present, and God shows Himself strong.

Like Samson's journey, which ultimately led him to stand before a massive gathering of God's enemies, Elijah's journey led him to a similar situation under different circumstances. Many would say of a famine or a drought—these are terrible things to endure! Yes, they are, but these pressing issues brought together many of the worst characters in Elijah's day. Elijah was in the wilderness up to this time, being protected and provided for until this fateful day when the Great God of heaven, unbeknownst to those attending, declared war on Jezebel and her minions.

Elijah set foot on Mount Carmel, and because of Elijah's directive—that Ahab would summon the people from all over Israel—it is likely that hundreds, if not thousands, came together on Mount Carmel for this spectacle. The nation was in a horrible famine, and desperation was likely the driving force behind everyone coming to Carmel. It is interesting to note that the Carmel Mountain range is 1,742 feet in elevation at its highest point, extending roughly 30 miles to the southeast of modern-day Haifa from the shores of the Mediterranean Sea. It comprises a beautiful series of curved peaks and valleys from which the sea can easily be seen. It was a geographically prominent location and, thus, a good setting for Elijah's contest. (It is unknown exactly where Elijah's confrontation played out.)[1]

AHAB THOUGHT THE ADVANTAGE WAS HIS

So Ahab sent unto all the children of Israel, and gathered the prophets together unto mount Carmel.

—1 Kings 18:20 KJV

The prophet of God, in the right strategic location, at the right time, and under divine orders, took his first steps into this mountain arena to face Jezebel's demonic horde. Imagine one man of God against these prophets of Baal, with an entire nation watching. If this were a modern-day scenario, it would likely be a live televised event with the whole world watching. Yet there they were, Elijah, gazing confidently at this occultic army.

Ahab agreed on Mount Carmel because he would have seen it as a fitting site since it was positioned between Israel and Phoenicia, the lands of the deities Ahab worshiped. Also, the Phoenicians regarded Mount Carmel as the sacred dwelling place of Baal. No doubt Ahab was highly pleased with this suggested site for the contest because, in Ahab's estimation, it would have given the prophets of Baal a definite advantage.

A MAN WITH A REVELATION IS NOT AT THE MERCY OF A CULTURE GONE MAD

And Elijah came unto all the people, and said, How long halt ye between two opinions? if the LORD be God, follow him: but if Baal, then follow him. And the people answered him not a word. 22 Then said Elijah unto the people, I, even I only, remain a prophet of the LORD; but Baal's prophets are four hundred and fifty men.

—1 Kings 18:21-22 KJV

When Elijah finally arrived, he told the crowd he was the only prophet of God remaining who would stand against these ungodly characters. Remember this: One man with a revelation from God is not at the mercy of a culture gone mad! Elijah, the man of God, had a revelation, and, in this instance, he would soon prove that he was the majority. The evildoers must have arrogantly thought that one way or another, *We will overwhelm Elijah.*

REFORMERS OFFER THE CULTURE A CHOICE

God's prophet Elijah addressed the onlookers by asking in 1 Kings 18:21, "'How long will you falter between two opinions? If the LORD is God, follow Him; but if Baal, follow him.' And the people answered him not a word." Elijah proposed the question, *Who will you follow,* and at this moment, the onlookers didn't answer him. Why? Because they had been under the rule of spiritual tyranny without any reprieve, leading to disillusionment. "When the righteous are in authority, the people rejoice; but when a wicked man rules, the people groan" (Proverbs 29:2).

One commentator translated it this way:

> "How long will you go hobbling between the two forks of the road?" Regardless of the translation, the meaning is still crystal clear: The issue was before the people; a clear decision was to be made! If Baal was to be God, Jehovah must be renounced. If Jehovah was to reign as God, Baal

and all his worship must be forever rejected and exchanged for a dedicated loyalty to Jehovah.[2]

WHAT REFORMERS SAY IS GOOD

When all the people had assembled, Elijah, the reformer of his generation, stood before them and challenged them to end their double-mindedness and to stop wavering between two opinions! It wasn't enough that he told the people they needed to choose. They needed more—a demonstration.

ELIJAH OFFERED THEM A DEMONSTRATION—THE GOD WHO ANSWERS BY FIRE!

"Then you call on the name of your gods, and I will call on the name of the LORD; and the God who answers by fire, He is God." So all the people answered and said, "It is well spoken."

—**1 Kings 18:24**

Notice the response when those gathered were given the opportunity to see a demonstration! Elijah proclaimed, "The God who answers by fire, He is God." When they heard this, rather than not answer him, the people said, "It is well spoken." Another translation says, "What you say is good!" Isn't that the cry of every generation? "If God is real, will someone please show Him to me or let Him demonstrate His power in our world?" A response of this nature is what so many desire to say but are unable to articulate until a reformer presents a challenge as Elijah did. Displays of God's power, or its potential, summon what is on the inside and call it to the forefront, the God part of an individual and a culture. Everyone is waiting for an encounter with God. They may not even know it, but Elijah's statement caught the crowd's attention because he offered a demonstration. When reformers show up, they don't attempt to win an argument; they simply show up with the power of demonstration!

REMEMBER THE WORDS OF THE APOSTLE PAUL

But I will come to you shortly, if the Lord wills, and I will know, not the word of those who are puffed up, but the power. [20] *For the kingdom of God is not in word but in power.*

—1 Corinthians 4:19-20

*For our gospel did not come to you in word only, but also **in power**, and in the Holy Spirit and in much assurance, as you know what kind of men we were among you for your sake.*

—1 Thessalonians 1:5

*And my speech and my preaching were not with persuasive words of human wisdom, but in **demonstration of the Spirit and of power**.*

—1 Corinthians 2:4

Power is required; raw Holy Spirit horsepower is a dinner bell to the world and a method by which God shakes the complacent out of their slumber. Notice Paul stated he did not come in speech. He was coming in demonstration! It is the power of God that confronts the hardened, fallow ground of a generation. Many pretend not to hear the Voice of God, yet an intersection with the God of the universe presented through a reformer will break the calloused veneer, even if it is momentarily. Power will give evil pause.

ELIJAH SET UP THE RULES
OF ENGAGEMENT

Then Elijah said to the people, "I alone am left a prophet of the LORD; but Baal's prophets are four hundred and fifty men. ²³ *Therefore let them give us two bulls; and let them choose one bull for themselves, cut it in pieces, and lay it on the wood, but put no fire under it; and I will prepare the other bull, and lay it on the wood, but put no fire under it.* ²⁴ *Then you call on the name of your gods, and I will call on the name of the LORD; and the God who answers by fire, He is God." So all the people answered and said, "It is well spoken."* ²⁵ *Now Elijah said to the prophets of Baal, "Choose one bull for yourselves and prepare it first, for you are many; and call on the name of your god, but put no fire under it."* ²⁶ *So they took the bull which was given them, and they prepared it, and called on the name of Baal from morning even till noon, saying, "O Baal, hear us!" But there was no voice; no one answered. Then they leaped about the altar which they had made.*

—1 Kings 18:22-26

Elijah had an understanding that the modern-day Church should take notice of. First, he was calling the shots. Why? Because he had a word from God. As I often say, "A man or woman with a word from God is not at the mercy of a culture going mad." Certainly, this was the case with Elijah, yet it must be stated Elijah was not acting presumptuously. Instead, he was bold at this moment, for he knew that God had spoken to him. Due to his word from God, he was fearless against the army of darkness standing before him. Modern believers are often timid and passive because right at the beginning of a matter, they are most often void of a word from the Lord.

Further, passivity is the go-to response without a word from the Lord. Our modern churches need a word from God, which will induce boldness to act, speak up, and even demonstrate to the unbelieving world.

REFORMERS SPEAK OUT SOMETIMES WITH SARCASM AGAINST EVIL!

And so it was, at noon, that Elijah mocked them and said, "Cry aloud, for he is a god; either he is meditating, or he is busy, or he is on a journey, or perhaps he is sleeping and must be awakened." [28] *So they cried aloud, and cut themselves, as was their custom, with knives and lances, until the blood gushed out on them.* [29] *And when midday was past, they prophesied until the time of the offering of the evening sacrifice. But there was no voice; no one answered, no one paid attention.*

—1 Kings 18:27-29

Have you ever considered why Elijah was so sarcastic regarding the false prophets and all the demonized voices standing in opposition to him? It was again due to having a word from God. One word from God changes the argument, fostering clarity unavailable to the opposing forces. God will cause those who hear Him to overcome the evil they are facing. Darkness has a voice; it says, "No, you can't, no, you won't. We will dominate you and your belief in the God you serve."

When faced with a scenario such as this, sarcasm will arise from a place of revelation. A better way of saying it would be that Elijah knew what would happen before he stepped into the battle arena. He was armed with confidence in God, and when he was exposed to their vile religious practices and ceremonies right before him, the prophet was honoring God by insulting those wicked characters.

Confidence arises from a place of revelation. A place of consecration that leads to demonstration with an ultimate glorification. Anything that gets in the way of that glorious end will be disesteemed, even mocked, by someone with a clear word from the Lord.

REFORMERS REPAIR HOLY RUINS

Then Elijah said to all the people, "Come near to me." So all the people came near to him. And he repaired the altar of the LORD that was broken down. [31] And Elijah took twelve stones, according to the number of the tribes of the sons of Jacob, to whom the word of the LORD had come, saying, "Israel shall be your name." [32] Then with the stones he built an altar in the name of the LORD; and he made a trench around the altar large enough to hold two seahs of seed. [33] And he put the wood in order, cut the bull in pieces, and laid it on the wood, and said, "Fill four waterpots with water, and pour it on the burnt sacrifice and on the wood." [34] Then he said, "Do it a second time," and they did it a second time; and he said, "Do it a third time," and they did it a third time. ³⁵ *So the water ran all around the altar; and he also filled the trench with water.* ³⁶ *And it came to pass, at the time of the offering of the evening sacrifice, that Elijah the prophet came near and said, "LORD God of Abraham, Isaac, and Israel, let it be known this day that You are God in Israel and I am Your servant, and that I have done all these things at Your word."*

—**1 Kings 18:30-36**

It is highly symbolic and even prophetic that the prophet rebuilt the former altar unto the Lord. Through this prophetic act, he was making a statement that God would once again be worshiped in His own land. Here, Elijah was fulfilling an assignment of prophets: restoring breaches and rebuilding ancient ruins. Isaiah 58:12 (KJV) says, "And they that shall be of thee shall build the old waste places: thou shalt raise up the foundations of many generations; and thou shalt be called, The repairer of the breach, The restorer of paths to dwell in."

REFORMERS USHER IN THE FIRE OF GOD

"Hear me, O LORD, hear me, that this people may know that You are the LORD God, and that You have turned their hearts back to You again." ³⁸ *Then the fire of the LORD fell and consumed the burnt sacrifice, and the wood and the stones and the dust, and it licked up the water that was in the trench.* ³⁹ *Now when all the people saw it, they fell on their faces; and they said, "The LORD, He is God! The LORD, He is God!"*

—**1 Kings 18:37-39**

Elijah not only made a declaration but was also present for its fulfillment. The God who answers by fire made good on Elijah's declaration. Hope was not deferred, so the people moved toward the Lord, falling on their faces in repentance and worship to admonish the Lord by saying, "He is God!"

REFORMERS EXECUTE JUDGMENT OF EVIL

And Elijah said to them, "Seize the prophets of Baal! Do not let one of them escape!" So they seized them; and Elijah brought them down to the Brook Kishon and executed them there.

—1 Kings 18:40

Justice is part of the responsibility of a bringer of reformation. In this case, after the miracle that turned the people's hearts back to God, justice had to be served against the agents of idolatry in the land. It is the responsibility of God's agent to do this and to aim for the judgment where it is due.

A point of interest is the location where justice was executed. The Brook of Kishon flows through the Valley of Megiddo. This ancient city is the same location where the battle of Armageddon will be fought. The final battle between good and evil where the ultimate act of justice will be served at the end of the age.

REFORMERS BRING THE RAIN

Then Elijah said to Ahab, "Go up, eat and drink; for there is the sound of abundance of rain." 42 *So Ahab went up to eat and drink. And Elijah went up to the top of Carmel; then he bowed down on the ground, and put his face between his knees, [43] and said to his servant, "Go up now, look toward the sea." So he went up and looked, and said, "There is nothing." And seven times he said, "Go again." [44] Then it came to pass the seventh time, that he said, "There is a cloud, as small as a man's hand, rising out of the sea!" So he said, "Go up, say to Ahab, 'Prepare your chariot, and go down before the rain stops you.'" [45] Now it happened in the meantime that the sky became black with clouds and wind, and there was a heavy rain. So Ahab rode away and went to Jezreel. [46] Then the hand of the LORD came upon Elijah; and he girded up his loins and ran ahead of Ahab to the entrance of Jezreel.*

—**1 Kings 18:41-46**

At the end of it all, the declaration, the sarcasm, the fire, and the judgment bring blessings to the land. Elijah ushered in the blessing of rain. First, removing what was blocking the Lord's blessing had to be confronted, and then came the rain.

We are in a war for the hearts of a generation. That is why Elijah came to his generation. That is why you are reading this right now. To confront the spirit of Antichrist (I will discuss this in detail in the pages ahead) and raise the next round of believers!

WE MUST PARTICIPATE

How can we participate? What can we do to make a difference? The answer is to do what we can, where we can, and as we can. Obeying and doing the work of God is vital. It can be prayer, raising children in the knowledge of the Lord, or consistency with a job to influence those in your orbit. Sometimes, it's to reach *the one* in your sphere of influence and bring them to know who Jesus is. Regarding *one*—consider this next story, for often, we view effectiveness in the kingdom through a subjective lens. It is simply our obedience that matters most.

THE IMPACT OF ONE

When it comes to contemporary heroes of the Christian faith, we are familiar with names like Billy Graham. But what about Edward Kimble or Mordecai Ham?

Edward Kimble was a shoe salesman who worked alongside a guy named Dwight. Edward shared the gospel with Dwight, and Dwight accepted Christ. It was 1858, and Dwight's last name was Moody. We know him as D. L. Moody, who was one of the greatest evangelists in history.

Years later, when Moody was preaching, a pastor named Frederick D. Meyer was deeply stirred, and as a result, he went into his own nationwide preaching ministry. On one occasion, when Meyer was preaching, a college student named J. Wilbur Chapman heard him and accepted Christ. He went out and began to share the gospel, and he employed a young baseball player named Billy Sunday. Billy Sunday ended up being the greatest evangelist of his generation.

When Billy Sunday preached the gospel in Charlotte, North Carolina, it was such a great meeting that he was invited back. But when he couldn't be there, Sunday recommended a preacher named Mordecai Ham. Ham went to Charlotte and preached, but not many people responded to his invitation to accept Christ. But on one of the last nights, a tall, lanky boy who worked on the local dairy farm walked forward. Everyone knew him as Billy Frank—we know him today as Billy Graham.

So Edward Kimble reached D. L. Moody, who touched Frederick Meyer, who reached Wilbur Chapman, who helped Billy Sunday, who reached businessmen in Charlotte, who invited Mordecai Ham, who ultimately reached Billy Graham. And it all began with the simple witness of Edward Kimble.[3]

How do we change the world? One simple act of faithfulness at a time.

CHAPTER TWO

THE WITCH
AND HER
UNSCRUPULOUS KING

And it came to pass, as though it had been a trivial thing for him to walk in the sins of Jeroboam the son of Nebat, that he took as wife Jezebel the daughter of Ethbaal, king of the Sidonians; and he went and served Baal and worshiped him.

—**1 Kings 16:31**

Jezebel's arrival on the scene was a journey filled with idolatry. She was a vile character based on her infamous behavior toward the nation and the prophets of God. It would not be a far stretch to say she was demonically possessed because of her lifelong dedication to the worship of the satanic entity Baal—who, for all purposes, is one of the personas of Satan in the Old Testament. Jezebel's rise to infamy began with her father, and her rise to power was realized through Ahab, her husband. Not only was Ahab marrying an idolatrous heathen, but he was authorizing a queen to rule who openly practiced idolatry and persecuted anyone practicing the things of God. She was hideously cruel, and among her many treacheries, she put to death the prophets and priests of God.

Ethbaal, Jezebel's father, identified with the Ithobalus of Menander, who reigned in Tyre, probably over all

Phoenicia, within 50 years of the death of Hiram. This Ithobalus, whose name means "With him is Baal," was originally a priest of the great temple of Astarte in Tyre. At the age of 36, he conspired against the Tyrian king, Pheles (a usurping fratricide), killed him, and seized the throne. His reign lasted 32 years, and he established a dynasty which continued on the throne at least 62 years longer.[1]

We see that Jezebel originated from an *occult background*. Her father was named after Baal, a moniker again attached to the Old Testament persona of Satan. Ancient historian Josephus, writing many centuries later, describes Jezebel's father as a priest of the goddess Astarte, who had usurped the throne.

EVIL UNION OF AHAB AND QUEEN JEZEBEL

In the thirty-eighth year of Asa king of Judah, Ahab the son of Omri became king over Israel; and Ahab the son of Omri reigned over Israel in Samaria twenty-two years. [30] Now Ahab the son of Omri did evil in the sight of the LORD, more than all who were before him. [31] And it came to pass, as though it had been a trivial thing for him to walk in the sins of Jeroboam the son of Nebat, that he took as wife Jezebel the daughter of Ethbaal, king of the Sidonians; and he went and served Baal and worshiped him. [32] Then he set up an altar for Baal in the temple of Baal, which he had built in Samaria. [33] And Ahab made a wooden image. Ahab did more to provoke the LORD God of Israel to anger than all the kings of Israel who were before him. [34] In his days Hiel of Bethel built Jericho. He laid its foundation with Abiram his firstborn, and with his youngest son Segub he set up its gates, according to the word of the LORD, which He had spoken through Joshua the son of Nun.

—1 Kings 16:29-34

King Ahab took Jezebel, an idolatrous heathen, as his wife. He authorized her to rule openly with her idolatry.

Now it happened, when Joram saw Jehu, that he said, "Is it peace, Jehu?" So he answered, "What peace, as long as the harlotries of your mother Jezebel and her witchcraft are so many?"

—2 Kings 9:22

FATHER AND MOTHER OF EVIL

Jezebel and Ahab represent the perversion and inversion of everything Elijah was representing. Ahab and Jezebel were a twisted version of father and mother to the nation. Although they were evil, due to the office they stood in, they were indeed the parental figures of the land. When considering this, it is crucial to understand that the devil will attempt to fill in areas of authority through dark figures of authority, especially if the righteous do not fill those seats. In the case of Elijah, a prophet of generational purpose, a true father to the land, he was the legitimate compared to the counterfeit in office at that time. In the pages ahead, we will look at Elijah's generational purpose.

AHAB WAS THE WORST OF
THIS WICKED DUO

In many ways, even considering the atrocities Jezebel induced and carried out during her tenure, as bad as she was, Ahab was worse. Please let me explain.

Ahab, who bore the king's responsibility rather than doing what was right in the eyes of the Lord, operated as a *polluted well* that defiled his station.

> *A righteous man who falters before the wicked is like a murky spring and a polluted well.*
>
> **—Proverbs 25:26**

King Ahab married Jezebel, built a temple, and made an altar for Baal. Additionally, the corrupt king established the worship of Asherah, the Sidonian Venus.

Omri was succeeded by his son Ahab, whose eventful reign of upwards of twenty years occupies so large a space even in these fragmentary records. His name means "brother-father" and has probably some sacred reference. He is stigmatized by the historians as a king more wicked than his father, though Omri had "done worse than all who were before him." That he was a brave warrior and showed some great qualities during a long and on the whole prosperous career; that he built cities, and added to Israel yet another royal residence; that he advanced the wealth and prosperity of his subjects; that he was highly successful in some of his wars against Syria, and died in battle against those dangerous enemies of his country; that he maintained unbroken, and strengthened by yet closer affinity, the recent alliance with the Southern Kingdom, --all this goes for nothing with the prophetic annalists. They have no word of eulogy for the king who added Baal-worship to the sin of Jeroboam. The prominence of Ahab in their record is only due to the fact that he came into dreadful collision with the prophetic order, and with Elijah, the greatest prophet who had yet arisen. The glory and the sins of the warrior-king interested the young prophets of the schools solely because they were interwoven with the grand and somber traditions of their mightiest reformer.[2]

Among the issues that made Ahab a terrible leader was that he served and worshiped Baal. Perversely, it is certain that to his death Ahab continued to recognize Jehovah. He enshrined the name of Jehovah in the names of his children. In Ahab's situational ethics and moral flexibility, he consulted the prophets of Jehovah while being married to the very murderer (Jezebel) of Jehovah's prophetic order.

AHAB, AN UNSCRUPULOUS KING

Ahab represents the worst kind of leader because he stands for anything that would bring him gain. His duplicity and maneuvering are all signs of narcissistic behavior. On the one hand, he was good at being in a relationship with God's people, while on the other, he was very comfortable working closely with pagan evil.

He only stood up for his desires. He gladly shook hands with the darkness, and in the same action, he would affiliate with the godly. Elijah's words in 1 Kings 18:21, "How long will you falter between two opinions? If the LORD is God, follow Him; but if Baal, follow him," was as much for the ears of Ahab as any of the people.

After the confrontation on Mount Carmel, Ahab supported Elijah for a time. For it was Ahab who would have consented to the killing of the prophets of Baal and the prophets who ate at Jezebel's table. When the prophet of God, Elijah, called for the killing of those wicked priests and prophets, Ahab, as king, could have lifted his voice and opposed Elijah. Ahab, agreeing with Elijah, displayed a severe flip-flop on a monumental issue! Ahab and Elijah were talking when Elijah said to the king "I hear the sound of the abundance of rain." Ahab was nearby!

It was not long after the events that brought about the miracle of rain back to the land that Jezebel threatened Elijah, and he fled. The question is, where was Ahab? He likely just went along with his demonized wife, flip-flopping once again.

Ahab represents situational morality, ethics, relationships, and alliances. He was a user for his gain. He would shift and change with the weather if it benefited him. In his mind, everything in Ahab's life was all about him.

THE SPIRIT OF AHAB

A true demon spirit gatekeeper seeks to embody individuals with positions of authority who are compromisers, such as Ahab. Ahab was far worse than Jezebel; he had authored governmental power over a nation and given Jezebel free reign to do as she wished. Worse yet, he participated. Ahab was very selfish and wanted to be liked by all sides of the aisle.

He is like the one who only wants what he wants and will use anyone or anything to get it. Often, these types are in business and politics; at times, they are the head of church organizations or any seat of power. As stated earlier, the spirit of Ahab will use anyone or anything to get what it wants, including God, political alliances, dark powers, Jezebel, and, if possible, the prophets or even Elijah. Ahab has the following characteristics:

+ He held authority.
+ Self-centered—the only side he was on was his own.
+ He tried to be friendly with the prophets and Jezebel's wishes.
+ He operated as a beta male to Jezebel.
+ He allowed Jezebel's witchcraft into the land through his seat of authority.
+ He was weak.
+ He complained.
+ He shifted the blame.
+ He was greedy.
+ He was passive-aggressive.

JEZEBEL INFLUENCED THE NATION

Being the new queen and using the authority given by Ahab. There are several ways that she influenced the nation:

1. She was the daughter of an idolatrous king and practiced idolatry and demonic arts openly.
2. She protected her vile religion and gave its partisans honors and rewards.
3. She used every means to persecute the prophets.
4. She had zero remorse and acted with the most zeal, perseverance, and relentless cruelty.

THAT WOMAN JEZEBEL IN THYATIRA

An example is in the book of Revelation, where Jesus addressed the church of Thyatira. Revelation 2:20, "Nevertheless I have a few things against you, because *you allow that woman Jezebel*, who calls herself a prophetess, to teach and seduce My servants to commit sexual immorality and eat things sacrificed to idols." In this passage of scripture the terminology, "to the angel" is used. When speaking of the "angel" this was a reference to the pastor of the church in Thyatira. Jezebel in this passage, amazingly enough, the two oldest manuscripts of the early Church read "your wife" talking to the pastor of the church, instead of "that woman." If so, this would mean that Jezebel of Thyatira was the pastor's wife! Now, please know the spirit of Jezebel is not a gender identifier. It is a spirit that will work through anyone who will cooperate with it. Additionally, it is very important to recognize that pastor's wives are heroes! Women in ministry are a vital part of the Church. This particular issue of Jezebel is not a reflection in any way on the godly women who serve in the Church, especially pastor's wives![3]

Calling this woman in Thyatira "Jezebel" gives more insight into who Jezebel was and how it operates, specifically when that same operation occurs in our time. Jezebel here is identified by Jesus. If Jesus Himself calls a person Jezebel, we should consider what He refers to.[4]

JEZEBEL CALLED HERSELF A PRIESTESS

Jezebel often disguises herself as prophetic. Why? Because she craves spiritual authority or power over people. A title like a prophet or prophetess gives the figure of Jezebel a moniker or title of prestige and the ability to speak as if she had a special revelation. Knowing that the instance in Thyatira references the pastor's wife suggests she pretended to hear from God.

After all, she was in church leadership. When working with leaders and their vision, there are times when the leadership in the church or ministry they represent has difficult people around them. They want to hold the leader's feet to the fire at every turn, almost as if they are the principal or great OZ in control, and the visionary leader must get permission and ask them for everything. Please understand that I love accountability and celebrate good leadership and healthy boards and deacons, yet when leaders cannot even breathe or carry out the vision because they have been wholly caged in by those they have around them, I label that ministry or church "deacon possessed."

Visionaries and leaders certainly need accountability and healthy figures of biblical structure around them, but not deacon possession. In the case of Jezebel, the leadership of a church or ministry goes well beyond deacon possession and jumps the tracks right into demonic activity set out to destroy the church.

JEZEBEL TAUGHT IN THE CHURCH

No wonder Jezebel persuaded members to act out in such horrible ways. Whatever a believer listens to, more of that will be given to them. Teaching is a place of significant influence in the body of Christ. No wonder James 3:1 states, "My brethren, let not many of you become teachers, knowing that we shall receive a stricter judgment." If that applies to those desiring the office of a teacher, imagine the judgment a false teacher/prophet would face from God!

JEZEBEL SEDUCED THE PEOPLE OF GOD

The word "seduce" in Greek is *planáō* and means *wandering* or *cause to wander, lead, or cause to go astray*. Similar to this reference in Revelation 2:20, to seduce and cause wandering, is Matthew 24:11, where

Jesus warned of false prophets. That they would come and deceive many. One of the Greek meanings is to *cause to wander* in that reference *to deceive many*. You can see the parallels between seduction and the activity of false prophets. Again, this points to why Jezebel wanted to carry the title of "prophetess" for power.

Many times, when someone hears the word "seduce," they immediately think it refers to a sexual enticement from something or someone. Although that would be an accurate use of the word, that is not its foundational meaning. Simply, it means *to distract or take someone off their assignment.*

THE RICH YOUNG RULER WAS SEDUCED

Seduction is taking a person on the path of life who is walking in their purpose and pulling them off. We see this in the story of Samson, with Delilah, or a similar school of thought could be seen in the narrative of the *rich young ruler*. Money was too much of an appeal for the rich young ruler, and he could not follow Jesus when asked to give it up and follow. His money would be an example of a type of seduction. Here, though, we see Jezebel did entice and seduce church people into actions that would take them away from God.

JEZEBEL OFFERED THEM AN AVENUE OR ENCOURAGEMENT TO SEXUAL IMMORALITY

Jezebel will always have a seduction to it that permits sexual immorality. Revelation 2:20 says, she taught. She was a teacher in the church from a place of authority. This demonized figure fulfilled the desire that Jezebel always seeks to induce by using the platform to teach sexual immorality. In this case, what was being taught here must have been some grace-gone-mad teaching, which likely said, do whatever you like, push the boundaries. It's ok with God! Then, she likely took it another step and directly encouraged them to take steps into those unsanctioned sexual activities.

FALSE PROPHETS HAVE SIMILAR DOCTRINE

Interestingly, one false prophet's behavior can be like another. Balaam, or the doctrine of Balaam, caused the children of Israel to do the same things Jezebel taught in her church sessions! Balaam did the same thing as mentioned in Revelation 2:14: "...you have there those who hold the doctrine of Balaam, who taught Balak to put a stumbling block before the children of Israel, to eat things sacrificed to idols, and to commit sexual immorality."

Additionally, the doctrine of the Nicolaitans, in Revelation 2:6, says, "But this you have, that you hate the deeds of the Nicolaitans, which I also hate." Revelation 2:15 says, "Thus you also have those who hold the doctrine of the Nicolaitans, which thing I hate."

Some scholars believe the Nicolaitans came from Nicolas, a proselyte of Antioch (Acts 6:5) who was first a Greek or Gentile and then became a Jew, a proselyte of righteousness, a Christian, and finally a deacon. Some think that from this man sprung the sect of the Nicolaitans, spoken of in Revelation 2. Nicolas—whose name means "one who conquers the people," was possibly one of the deacons of the early Church mentioned in Acts 6:5. Some suggest that it is possible Nicolas became an apostate, denying the true faith and practiced "the doctrine of Balaam," a false prophet who taught Israel "to sin by eating food sacrificed to idols and by committing sexual immorality" (Revelation 2:14).[5]

I have included a reference from early church history to the Nicolaitans, who operated in the doctrine of Balaam:

"They abandoned themselves to pleasure like goats, leading a life of self-indulgence." Their teaching perverted grace and replaced liberty with license.

—Clement of Alexandria

TWISTED SCRIPTURE

These three clowns, Jezebel, Nicolas, and Balaam should've started a band in the style and flavor of an '80s rock band called "Twisted Sister." Only their band would have a name more fitting to them…it would be called Twisted Scripture!

Their title hit song would be "We're not gonna teach truth, no! We're not gonna teach the truth. We're not gonna teach truth anymore!" With the follow-up verse that would proudly sing, "We're on the road to perdition, yeah! The road to perdition, we are gonna burn, yeah, for all time!"

I just needed to add that piece of humor—Dear reader, you're welcome.

JEZEBEL LIKEWISE ENCOURAGED OR OFFERED A PATH TO EATING THINGS SACRIFICED TO IDOLS

Paul discusses this issue in 1 Corinthians 10:25-31.

Eat whatever is sold in the meat market, asking no questions for conscience' sake; 26 for "the earth is the Lord's, and all its fullness." 27 If any of those who do not believe invites you to dinner, and you desire to go, eat whatever is set before you, asking no question for conscience' sake.

²⁸ But if anyone says to you, "This was offered to idols," do not eat it for the sake of the one who told you, and for conscience' sake; for "the earth is the Lord's, and all its fullness." ²⁹ "Conscience," I say, not your own, but that of the other. For why is my liberty judged by another man's conscience? ³⁰ But if I partake with thanks, why am I evil spoken of for the food over which I give thanks? ³¹ Therefore, whether you eat or drink, or whatever you do, do all to the glory of God.

—1 Corinthians 10:25-31

However, Paul instructed that it should not be eaten for the sake of conscience—not his own or to the mature; instead, Paul was speaking of the conscience of others. Idol sacrifice would carry an association with pagan idolatry, and if someone was newly coming into the church, such an act could hurt their conscience. In this instance, Jezebel was attempting to corrupt the conscience of church members.

Jezebel was teaching accommodation for the church of Thyatira so that the people could intermingle with all the world's ways and idolatry of that region.

JEZEBEL WAS ALLOWED— SHE HAD PERMISSION

She was allowed to operate under the church's leadership, which is very revealing. This means her husband, who was the pastor, must have been an Ahab figure who allowed Jezebel to do whatever she wanted in that church. Often, it is not only the evil force that is to blame for demonic activity, but equally, it is the silent consent of the leadership, who, like a trodden-through puddle, allows vile behavior to thrive.

THE ISSUE OF A GUILTY CONSCIENCE IS A MECHANISM USED BY JEZEBEL AND FALSE PROPHETS

And by this we know that we are of the truth, and shall assure our hearts before Him. [20] For if our heart condemns us, God is greater than our heart, and knows all things. [21] Beloved, if our heart does not condemn us, we have confidence toward God.

—1 John 3:19-21

First John 3:19-21 helps understand the scope and lens of the entire situation. It is summed up in this: *if your heart condemns you, God is greater than your heart!* Just imagine walking in holiness and a cleansed conscience to such a degree that you see God's love for you for what it is—beyond measure! A wonderful revelation is recognizing God's will for us and drawing near Him with full assurance! "Let us draw near with a true heart in full assurance of faith, having our hearts sprinkled from an evil conscience and our bodies washed with pure water" (Hebrews 10:22).

The condemnation of the devil working through figures like this woman, Jezebel, stalls out or paralyzes a believer. Why? Because they corrupt their conscience. Notice that God never changes, but the believer changes based on their beliefs about themselves or God. The battle is not over whether God loves you or if He accepts you. The battle is over how you perceive these things based on what you have allowed into your heart.

THE SPIRIT OF JEZEBEL

In modern Christianity, the catchphrase is "the spirit of Jezebel." The Jezebel spirit is a demon, and it seems to have a variety of subjective meanings that can alternate based on who is talking about it. Terminology is important as these kinds of names and labels can be very destructive when aimed at people. Often, it may be that a person does not like an individual or may have experienced a negative encounter with them, thus labeling them Jezebel. Having said that, it is important to remember that scripturally speaking, it was Jesus who gave the woman in Revelation 2:20 the title "Jezebel." Which then sets a precedent. If Jesus said it, then it is worth looking at.

CHARACTERISTICS OF A JEZEBEL SPIRIT

In the case of Jezebel, we must consider her characteristics, not only her but also the Jezebel Jesus referenced in Revelation. Demon spirits will work through people susceptible to Jezebel's influence and characteristics. Therefore, the Jezebel spirit is nothing more than a demon influencing a person, causing them to act as closely as possible to Jezebel. Scripture lays out for us how Jezebel operated by what she did in the Bible, both the first Jezebel and the woman Jesus referred to as Jezebel in Revelation 2:20:

+ She calls herself a prophetess but is a witch.
+ Hates real prophets.
+ She surrounds herself with false prophets.
+ Claims to be a teacher.
+ Teaches sexual immorality.
+ Seduces the people of God to disobey God.

- ✦ Seduces the people of God into sexual behavior with her.

- ✦ Encourages compromise to the laws of God.

- ✦ Filled with rage.

- ✦ She has a desire to murder her enemies.

- ✦ Manipulates for her agenda to control.

- ✦ She has emasculated weak men around her.

- ✦ Surrounds herself with sexually altered eunuchs or transgenders.

Characteristics of a Jezebel demon can be identified by patterns in an individual's life or discerned by the Holy Spirit. Make sure, however, not to jump to conclusions. Many people have been damaged by the overzealous and super spiritual individuals who quickly throw out the label "Jezebel." Be sure to walk with mature believers filled with God's love and rooted in the Word of God. Do not be quick to throw out these terms when dealing with people and their behaviors. Walk circumspectly and in the Holy Spirit by praying in the Spirit.

If you feel you are in a battle with the spirit of Jezebel, then pray. God will answer you. Knowing that any spirit can be bound, but spirits that are at home with a host who does not want to cooperate with the things of God makes casting it out difficult.

THE JEZEBEL DEMON STILL OPPOSES ELIJAH TODAY

Jezebel was the leading force against Elijah and is a major factor in resisting the spirit of Elijah today. We see in 1 Kings 18:4 that Jezebel was killing prophets of God! Whoever the demon could not kill among the prophets, it would *intimidate*.

Imagine it! In her day, Jezebel intimidated the prophets of the living God to the point that they hid from her. Many legitimate prophets are hiding today from the same spirit of intimidation when they should be rising and speaking out on various issues.

The evil spirit even went as far as to threaten, and effectively so, the most recognized prophet of the day. First Kings 19:2 says, "Then Jezebel sent a messenger to Elijah, saying, 'So let the gods do to me, and more also, if I do not make your life as the life of one of them by tomorrow about this time.'"

Jezebel declared herself to be the voice of God or a prophet. She thought her voice was equal to Elijah's because she believed she was a prophetess. She even placed occultic practitioners on the payroll in her kingdom and had them eat at her table.

JEZEBEL WAS TERRITORIAL, CULTURALLY DOMINANT

Much can be learned from her behavior to better understand the issues arising in our day.

> The new queen inherited the fanaticism as she inherited the ferocity of her father. She acquired from the first a paramount sway over the weak and uxorious mind of her husband under her influence Ahab built in Samaria a splendid temple and altar to Baal, in which no less than four hundred orgiastic priests served the Phoenician idol in splendid vestments, and with the same pompous ritual as in the shrines at Tyre. In front of this temple, to the disgust and horror of all faithful worshippers of Jehovah, stood an Asherah in honor of the Nature-goddess, and Matstseboth pillars or obelisks which represented either

sunbeams or the reproductive powers of nature. In these ways Ahab "did more to provoke the Lord God to anger than all the kings of Israel that were before him." {1Ki 16:23; 2Ki 3:2; 2Ki 10:27}[6]

VILE BAAL WORSHIP WAS INTRODUCED AND ELEVATED IN THE NATION

Who and what was Baal? When we learn what Baal was and how he was worshiped, it is not surprising that God's fiery condemnation followed. Baal's appearance was half sun-god, half Bacchus, and half Hercules.

Baal was also worshiped under the image of a bull, "the symbol of the male power of generation." Similar to the vile acts of worship to Peor and Moloch was the demand for victims to be sacrificed in horrible consecration of lust and blood. Baal also resembled the Minotaur, a figure known to some as the wallowing "infamy of Crete," a name given because of its required yearly tribute of youths and maidens.

From descriptions of Jezebel and Ahab's temple at Apheka, scholars learned of Jezebel's devotion to Baal and Asherah. Wealthy gifts were abundant, and a multitude of priests, women, and mutilated ministers would gather in splendid vestments.

CHILD SACRIFICE AND TRANSSEXUALITY WERE PART OF WORSHIP

Children were sacrificed in these pagan ceremonies by being put in a leather bag and flung down from the top of the temple, with the shocking expression that "they were calves, not children."

In the forecourt of these places of worship stood two gigantic phalli. History tells us that the Galli (a eunuch priest) were maddened into a tumult of excitement by the uproar of drums, shrill pipes, and clanging cymbals, gashed themselves with knives and potsherds, and often ran through the city in women's dresses. These Galli were those who castrated themselves during ecstatic celebrations, becoming eunuchs. They performed dances to the music of pipes and tambourines and, in ecstasy, flogged themselves until they bled.

They were presented as wearing bright clothes, heavy jewelry, makeup, and sporting bleached and crimped hair. Because the Galli castrated themselves and wore women's clothing, accessories, and makeup, some modern scholars have interpreted them as ancient writers, astrologers, and Christian apologists. Julius Firmicus Maternus said, "They say they are not men...they want to pass as women." He elaborated, "Animated by some sort of reverential feeling, they actually have made this element [air] into a woman. For, because air is an intermediary between sea and sky, they honor it through priests who have womanish voices."

These Galli, or eunuch worshipers, likely had ties to what is known as Cybele's cult, which may have originated in Mesopotamia and arrived in Greece around 300 BC.[7]

AHAB REBUILDS THE CURSED CITY!

Such was the new worship with which the dark murderess Jezebel insulted faith in Jehovah God. A consequence of this tolerance of polluted forms of worship greatly came to light when her unscrupulous husband, Ahab, defied Joshua's words who had pronounced a curse upon the city's site. Joshua proclaimed Jericho was never to be rebuilt but to remain under God's ban.

JOSHUA'S CURSE

Joshua had pronounced a curse on anyone who would rebuild the city of Jericho. Many interpreters have thought that a practice of the day was that the dedication of a house would feature the sacrifice of a child from the family. This was used to explain the skeletal remains of children found buried under the thresholds of houses (foundation sacrifices). Similarly, the builder of a city would sacrifice a child who would be buried in a significant location in the city.

Interestingly, this interpretation has been largely abandoned, and some researchers now see a connection between the curse and the disease schistosomiasis (bilharziasis). This disease is caused by a blood fluke carried by snails of the type found in abundance at Jericho. It infects the urinary tract and affects fertility and child mortality.[8]

THE ONLY ANSWER TO DARKNESS IS LIGHT!

When darkness reigns and evil, forbidden territory is being resurrected, much like Ahab resurrects Jericho, the children of the Most High Living God are to stand up to such an evil onslaught. Those who know, are awake, and understand what is happening in their generation must act! Preachers and ministers must act. God's people must act!

Jezebel stands out on the page of sacred history as the first supporter of religious persecution. She is the authentic originator of priestly inquisitions.

There are indications that Jezebel had gone further still and that Ahab, even if he may secretly have disapproved, had not interfered to stop her. We do not know the exact period at which Jezebel began to exercise violence against the worshipers of Jehovah, but certainly, she did so. This crime occurred before the great famine, which Elijah prophesied into the land appointed for punishment and rebuke. By Jezebel's idolatrous establishments, she tried to crush Jehovah's worship altogether.

One expositor referenced Jezebel as the source for other heinous crimes in recent history and where it leads if priests and prophets do not resist.

> The Borgian monster, Pope Alexander VI, who founded the Spanish Inquisition, is the lineal inheritor of the traditions of Jezebel. Had Ahab done no more than Solomon had done in Judah, the followers of the true faith in Israel would have been as deeply offended as those of the Southern Kingdom.

> They would have hated a toleration which they regarded as wicked, because it involved moral corruption as well as the danger of national apostasy. Their feelings would have been even more wrathful than were stirred in the hearts of English Puritans when they heard of the Masses in the chapel of Henrietta Maria, or saw Father Petre gliding about the corridors of Whitehall. But their opposition was crushed with a hand of iron.

> Jezebel, strong in her entourage of no less than eight hundred and fifty priests, to say nothing of her other attendants, audaciously broke down the altars of Jehovah—even the lonely one on Mount Carmel—and endeavored so completely to extirpate all the prophets of Jehovah that Elijah regarded himself as the sole prophet that was left. Those who escaped her fury had to wander about in destitution, and to hide in dens and caves of the earth.

> The apostasy of Churches always creeps on apace, when priests and prophets, afraid of malediction, and afraid of

imperiling their worldly interests become cowards, opportunists, and timeservers, and not daring to speak out the truth that is in them, suffer the cause of spirituality and righteousness to go by default.

But "when Iniquity hath played her part, Vengeance, leaps upon the stage. The comedy is short, but the tragedy is long. The black guard shall attend upon you: you shall eat at the table of sorrow, and the crown of death shall be upon your heads, many glittering faces looking upon you."9

EVEN ON A BAD DAY, YOU ARE ANOINTED TO BE THE BEST THERE IS!

Truthfully, there is only one thing that can stop a generational assault by Jezebel, and it is men and women with a word from the Living God. By default, the *Ekklesia* (the Church) will stop the dominance of Jezebel or any other nefarious spiritual agenda to present itself upon the land.

After all, if you are in Christ, then you are salt and light. You are preserving this place until the Lord returns. What holds darkness back is a revelation! Who you are, what you have, and what you are called to do. When these things get a hold of your life as you read the Bible and get to know the Lord through His Word, you become an agent who will shift the circumstances you are walking into.

We are called to shine light in the darkness. The territory is already yours if you are in Christ, and as such, you must take on the mindset that understands that all things are yours and you are here to enforce what has been made available to you. Jesus came and took the keys of death, hell, and the grave. He also threw the devil out of his party here on earth. That's right. Darkness was having a hay day, believing they could not be stopped, that was until Jesus came as the last Adam with the mission to take back God's children from under the devil's domination along with the eventual taking back of all territory. Including the entire earth. One day, not even as much as an inch of ground will be owned, held, or possessed by darkness. It will all come under the Lordship of Jesus. Revelation 11:15 says, "Then the seventh angel sounded: And there were loud voices in heaven, saying, 'The kingdoms of this world have become the kingdoms of our Lord and of His Christ, and He shall reign forever and ever!'"

Our job is to preach the gospel, be a light, and stand up without fear in a system that wants to be owned by the Antichrist. Even as they try to intimidate the body of believers, we must rise as Elijah did, and as you are about to discover—Elisha, who carried out the will of God, was first given to Elijah.

HOW TO RESIST JEZEBEL

Resisting Jezebel is just like resisting any other evil that exalts itself against the knowledge of God, with a Jezebel spirit or familiar demon to her operation.

Jezebel represents a spirit of control and manipulation and ultimately will seek to control and destroy the prophets—an interesting point about spirits that tempt and seek to corrupt. Once a person gives in, the same demon that tempts and entices will wait to accuse and condemn the person. How evil, such a hateful thing going into a scenario and a hateful thing on the other side. Demonic forces, such as the Jezebel spirit, would attempt to get the followers of Jesus to compromise all by operating by rules and legalities.

Actions, words, and attitudes are important in a spiritual battle against Jezebel or demonic enticement. Words and actions are legal scenarios in the spirit. When they are resisted, no evil words of unbelief are spoken, and no actions are taken that line up with evil. These forces are church members' access to or jurisdiction over the life of a believer. Demonic things want too badly to get the believer to compromise in some way as it empowers them to take action legally. Every believer must combat this by constantly taking in the Word of God to renew their mind and sanctify their actions.

CAST THEM OUT

From the Old Testament era to the present day, we live in the function of Jezebel and Ahab. We will always rise to attack or resist what Elijah is anointed for. Generational restoration. How do you deal with evil spirits like them? Cast them out! The question is how? How do you cast out a demon like that? By sending in a reformer—the spirit of Elijah!

CHAPTER THREE

A GENERATION
AT WAR WITH GOD

Because, although they knew God, they did not glorify Him as God, nor were thankful, but became futile in their thoughts, and their foolish hearts were darkened. [22] Professing to be wise, they became fools, [23] and changed the glory of the incorruptible God into an image made like corruptible man—and birds and four-footed animals and creeping things. [24] Therefore God also gave them up to uncleanness, in the lusts of their hearts, to dishonor their bodies among themselves, [25] who exchanged the truth of God for the lie, and worshiped and served the creature rather than the Creator, who is blessed forever. Amen.

—Romans 1:21-25

A generation at war with God begins with progressively removing God from their thinking. Worse yet, this trait is passed down to the children of those who omit God from their minds. Tragically, where the knowledge of God is put to the side, which, according to Romans 1, is executed by not glorifying Him as God, rejecting thankfulness and embracing a sense of entitlement, this becomes the ground for hostility and war against God.

Sin is then allowed to reign in the seat where the things of God should be meditated on. From this posture, a culture deteriorates.

Romans 1:21-25 speaks regarding those who, although they knew God, *chose* to remove the knowledge of God from their minds. What transpires is blindness and hardening of the heart; from this position comes all kinds of vile behaviors and the accompanying judgment.

Verse 24 clearly states that God gives them over to the opposite of Him because they desire these wicked things. God will not override the will of anyone who chooses for or against Him. In the case of Romans 1:24, God gave them over to *what they wanted* since He was vacant in their minds. The antithesis of the Great God of heaven is every vile thing—uncleanness, lust in their hearts, leading to the dishonoring of their bodies. Verse 25 points out that these exchange the truth of God for the lie and worship and serve *the creature rather than the Creator.*

It is disgraceful for any generation to make this turn after having been built on a foundation of the knowledge of God. This means that if a culture once had godly principles and a national fear of the Lord only to degrade such a position to outright rejection of the Lord of Glory is the basis for cultural demise.

If one continues to wallow in this rejection of God, eventually, a hatred for God will rise—a generation that becomes hostile toward God's things. Ultimately, this type of generation will find itself at war with God. A generation at war with God is truly the result of those who regard worthless idols in place of the Lord.

Those who regard worthless idols forsake their own Mercy.

—Jonah 2:8

Generational rejection of the Lord leads to a society collapsing due to sowing and reaping toward the principles of darkness, such as the flesh and anti-biblical living. Yet no matter how far this goes, God is still willing to receive those who have rejected Him back to Himself.

Consider Nineveh! In Jonah's estimation, they were beyond his mercy, yet God wanted to show them mercy by sending His prophet. Disdain for Nineveh was all Jonah could muster when the Lord asked him to go. Why? Because the wickedness of Nineveh personally impacted Jonah.

> *So he prayed to the LORD, and said, "Ah, LORD, was not this what I said when I was still in my country? Therefore I fled previously to Tarshish; for I know that You are a gracious and merciful God, slow to anger and abundant in lovingkindness, One who relents from doing harm."*
>
> —Jonah 4:2

Jonah was greatly upset when Nineveh repented. His statements to the Lord reveal that he had previously fled to Tarshish. "For I know that You are a gracious and merciful God, slow to anger and abundant in lovingkindness, One who relents from doing harm." Jonah conveyed that he knew God would likely have mercy on these people.

This upset Jonah for several possible reasons.

> First, Nineveh was the capital city of Assyria, a ruthless and warlike people who were enemies of Israel. Nineveh's destruction would have been seen as a victory for Israel.
>
> Second, Jonah probably wanted to see Nineveh's downfall to satisfy his own sense of justice. After all, in Jonah's estimation, Nineveh deserved God's judgment.[1]

Some have suggested Jonah's hostility toward the people of Nineveh was that he possibly lost family or loved ones at the hands of the Ninevites. Whatever the reason, Jonah wanted them judged and destroyed—something they likely deserved.

Nineveh offers us a glimpse of what can happen if a culture turns to God. According to biblical history, there can be a dramatic turn and awakening back to the things of God. It may come in the form of a terrible event affecting everyone in the informed world, such as the September 11, 2001, attacks on the World Trade Center in New York. Throughout the days following came a softening of the culture in America; tenderness and compassion were even present on talk shows at the time. Sadly, through tragedy, a turning may take place. A crisis of any kind can bring about a turn. Yet more than any event or tenderizing of a culture via a painful event, what brings a clarion call is an anointed reformer who doesn't back down and is filled with boldness against adversity.

THE SPIRIT OF ANTICHRIST AND THE WAR FOR RECONCILIATION

*He will also go before Him **in the spirit and power of Elijah**, "to turn the hearts of the fathers to the children," and the disobedient to the wisdom of the just, to make ready a people prepared for the Lord.*

—**Luke 1:17**

Elijah is again coming to declare war on the spirit of this age! A heated collision arrives for every generation with the god of this world (Satan) and his wicked plans against each generation's current inhabitants of Earth. Accompanying the fallen angel are all the usual suspects—deception, destruction, perversion, and an insatiable need to rule the world through his elite puppets.

Ultimately, this generational pathway will come to its fullness and manifest the coming of a false messiah, the man of sin, the Antichrist. Today, we have not yet seen the full embodiment of the Antichrist. Rather, we see something far more elusive: the *spirit of Antichrist.*

Manipulating a nation's social structures and working individually with those under the shadow of its evil agenda worldwide.

DEFINING THE SPIRIT OF ANTICHRIST

Ever since the fall of man, there have been many false religions and ungodly belief systems that attempt to usurp the God of heaven and do things how they wish rather than serve and surrender to the Creator. Much of this is due to the nefarious activities of those mutinous fallen angels who acted according to their will rather than in alignment with God's will. That same spirit has flooded the earth, and we face it today—the *spirit of Antichrist.*

> *Little children, it is the last hour; and as you have heard that the **Antichrist is coming**, even now **many antichrists have come,** by which we know that it is the last hour.* [19] *They went out from us, but they were not of us; for if they had been of us, they would have continued with us; but they went out that they might be made manifest, that none of them were of us.* [20] *But you have an anointing from the Holy One, and you know all things.* [21] *I have not written to you because you do not know the truth, but because you know it, and that no lie is of the truth.* [22] *Who is a liar but he who denies that Jesus is the Christ? He is antichrist who denies the Father and the Son.* [23] *Whoever denies the Son does not have the Father either; he who acknowledges the Son has the Father also.* [24] *Therefore let that abide in you which you heard from the beginning. If what you heard from the beginning abides in you, you also will abide in the Son and in the Father.* [25] *And this is the promise that He has promised us—eternal life.* [26] *These things I have written to you concerning those who*

try to deceive you. ²⁷ But the anointing which you have received from Him abides in you, and you do not need that anyone teach you; but as the same anointing teaches you concerning all things, and is true, and is not a lie, and just as it has taught you, you will abide in Him.

—1 John 2:18-27

The actual man of sin, the Antichrist, is coming and will rise one day to deceive the nations (2 Thessalonians 2:3). Right now, many Antichrists have gone into the world. A demon spirit works through individuals who deny King Jesus and seek to deceive the world around us to stay away from receiving Jesus.

The spirit of Antichrist thrives on control and world domination. The ultimate goal is to turn all away from Jesus Christ and lead a worldwide rebellion. Although the man of sin, the literal Antichrist, may not be in power as you read this—it is the spirit, or the function of the Antichrist, empowered by the devil, which attempts to accomplish all the same things as the literal Antichrist.

Today, we face the spirit of Antichrist through a deceived and godless world that is in a state of rebellion against the things of God and His Word.

WE ARE FACING THE SPIRIT OF ANTICHRIST IN OUR CULTURE

Now as He sat on the Mount of Olives, the disciples came to Him privately, saying, "Tell us, when will these things be? And what will be the sign of Your coming, and of the end of the age?" ⁴ And Jesus answered and said to them: "Take heed that no one deceives you. ⁵ For many will come in My name, saying, 'I am the Christ,' and will deceive many. ⁶ And you will hear of wars and rumors of wars. See that you are not troubled; for all these things must come to pass, but the end is not yet. ⁷ For nation will rise against nation, and kingdom against kingdom. And there will be famines, pestilences, and earthquakes in various places. ⁸ All these are the beginning of sorrows."

—Matthew 24:3-8

Matthew 24:7 describes how things will be at the end of the age. Everything described: false christs, wars and rumors of wars, nation rising against nation, kingdom against kingdom, famines, pestilences, and earthquakes in various places. Verse 8 locates all these events with Jesus telling us where they are happening in the timeline by referring to it as the beginning of sorrows. Another way of saying it is these are birth pangs, much like a woman about to give birth.

WAR OF REFORMATION AGAINST THE SPIRIT OF ANTICHRIST

Little children, it is the last hour; and as you have heard that the Antichrist is coming, even now many antichrists have come, by which we know that it is the last hour.

—1 John 2:18

In response to this malevolent force is the war of reformation made by the clear-eyed, clear-minded reformers who stand in every generation and say to the darkness, "No! You Move!" These have a unique calling and walk separately, countering their society to call those lost in darkness into God's marvelous light. Many will receive a call from the

Lord to rise and answer the wickedness coming against our generation and our children—the *spirit of Elijah!*

God delights in sending His agents into the exact battle zone of corruption to show darkness who the real authority is and as a reminder that one day, the entirety of creation will be reformed under the rule of God and His Christ. No one displays this more than Jesus by taking back the devil's territory. Before he was the devil, he was Lucifer, and he had a physical mountain location from which he administered his duties. To understand the war, we must understand its beginning— the original throne of Lucifer.

DE-THRONING SATAN'S TERRITORY

You were the anointed cherub who covers; I established you; you were on the holy mountain of God; you walked back and forth in the midst of fiery stones.

—**Ezekiel 28:14**

Ezekiel 28:14 refers to Lucifer and his original location—the mountain of God. It also refers to the fact that Lucifer's rule was on the earth itself. This point is reinforced by recognizing that in every other place in the Bible where the words to describe this mountain are used, "Har Elohim" always refers to a literal, earthly mountain.

As referenced in Exodus 3:1, it refers to Horeb, where Moses saw the burning bush. Exodus 4:27 is where Moses and Aaron meet. Moses camped there in Exodus 18:5, and he climbed it to meet God in Exodus 24:13. It was where Elijah sought the Lord in 1 Kings 19:8. In every instance, it is used about a literal, earthly mountain.

My point is this: upon Lucifer losing his physical location and seat of authority on earth, he sought to gain it back by deceiving Adam.

Lucifer's plan was successful regarding Adam until he ran into the last Adam—Jesus, the Son of the Living God.[2]

Satan wanted to show Jesus that he, the devil, had again gained a vantage point from a mountain—a position Satan acquired from Adam when the man listened to the deceiver's voice over the Voice of God. In the following scriptures, we see that Satan wanted to enforce his dark reign on earth by tempting Jesus with quick access to ruling the nations—only under the devil's authority.

> Then the devil took Him up into the holy city, set Him on the pinnacle of the temple, [6] and said to Him, "If You are the Son of God, throw Yourself down. For it is written: 'He shall give His angels charge over you,' and, 'In their hands they shall bear you up, lest you dash your foot against a stone.'" [7] Jesus said to him, "It is written again, 'You shall not tempt the LORD your God.'" [8] Again, the devil took Him up on an exceedingly high mountain, and showed Him all the kingdoms of the world and their glory. [9] And he said to Him, "All these things I will give You if You will fall down and worship me."
>
> **—Matthew 4:5-9**

> Then the devil, taking Him up on a high mountain, showed Him all the kingdoms of the world in a moment of time. [6] And the devil said to Him, "All this authority I will give You, and their glory; for this has been delivered to me, and I give it to whomever I wish. [7] Therefore, if You will worship before me, all will be Yours."
>
> **—Luke 4:5-7**

JESUS SEIZED THE DEVIL'S TERRITORY

Notice in Luke 4:5-7 how the devil had a new mountain and the ability to take Jesus to the top of the pinnacle of the temple. At this time, the people of God had zero authority over the territory and power of the devil.

Something that must be realized is that the devil is territorial! He wants territory and wishes to pervert the ways of God by reigning over all the territory he can dominate and have slaves do his bidding within his wicked domain. Opposite is the kingdom of God, which Jesus came to deliver those who believe in His name, creating a territory for His will to be done on earth as it is in heaven. Sons and daughters are the ones who do the will of God by preaching the gospel of the kingdom.

> "Now is the judgment of this world; now the ruler of this world will be cast out. [32] And I, if I am lifted up from the earth, will draw all peoples to Myself." [33] This He said, signifying by what death He would die.
>
> —John 12:31-33

Jesus was saying that He was taking back the territory, and the current ruler of this world was about to be cast out. How? By being lifted on the Cross and paying the ultimate sacrifice. Upon paying the price required to win the ability to bring those who receive Him back to the Father, Jesus additionally gained back all authority in heaven and on earth.

> And Jesus came and spoke to them, saying, "All authority has been given to Me in heaven and on earth."
>
> —Matthew 28:18

Jesus had completely thrown the devil out of his own party! As His Body, we are to preach the gospel and influence every corner of the physical world.

HOW IS THE DEVIL STILL HERE IF JESUS WON?

If Jesus kicked the devil out, why is it that we are dealing with so much darkness in the world? The devil is still around and very active. However, he no longer has the same territory he once did. The part that the body of Christ often does not realize is that just because the devil is defeated and cast out doesn't mean that he cannot steal, kill, and destroy through influencing unbelievers and the ungodly of this world.

Yes, Jesus won and seized the territory. A better way of saying it is that Jesus broke the devil's absolute control over the earth and its territories, now making it possible for us to drive out demons and dominate any territory through preaching the gospel and the influence of God's kingdom. Types and shadows of this are all over the Old Testament, especially in the Exodus, the conquest of Joshua, and when the people of God were given the promised land but had to go in, possess it, and then occupy it.

The same can be said regarding our lives in this world. Jesus gave us the authority to go in, occupy, and possess the land. However, today, it is done through influence and winning the hearts and minds of humanity over to the Lordship of Jesus. Wherever we do not bring influence and the gospel, the devil will, by default, take control by influencing unbelievers to enforce his evil kingdom. Where we don't go and execute the *Great Commission* (going into the world and winning the lost to Jesus) is where darkness will set up shop. This includes all the vile demonic spirits that have worked through evil characters from the ancient days, which is why you can see a pattern of the same types of demons working through willing individuals in each generation until they run into the kingdom of God, which mature believers are enforcing.

ANCIENT DEMONS MUST BE DRIVEN OUT!

Until the end of the age, we will be facing demonic strongholds over territories through human puppets of the devil. Although he has no authority over God's people and no longer owns territory—what he does have is highly effective! The devil has the seductive power of persuasion over the unbelieving; through them, he can still exercise his desires upon humanity. He is cast out but can still greatly impact society through free moral agents who do not know Jesus or, worse, are in rebellion against the things of God.

Of all the things we as believers must begin to realize is just how crucial it is that we:

1. Preach the gospel.

2. Influence every part of society because God cannot simply do it without His Body. As 1 John 4:17 says, "…as He is, so are we in this world."

This leads us to recognize what we are dealing with. It is not demons whisking through the unseen in front of us or around us, causing havoc. Rather, it is the battle to stop the weaponization of the hearts and minds of free moral agents before they become workers of the devil in this territory we all live in.

We are in an all-out war against the powers of darkness. Not head-on against these unseen wispy forces floating around in the invisible realm. Instead, we contend with them through their avatars. Those who are submitted to the will of hell. Those of corrupt minds operate by near remote control of these malevolent forces. That is the daily battle, the crux, the war we face. Loving our enemies, bringing the gospel to a demonized world, and influencing hearts and actions pave the way for many to see and hear the goodness of God in the land of the living.

> *For we do not wrestle against flesh and blood, but against principalities, against powers, against the rulers of the darkness of this age, against spiritual hosts of wickedness in the heavenly places.*
>
> **—Ephesians 6:12**

Our fight is not with flesh and blood. It is not the people we are fighting but the forces driving them. This is why you, doing your part and taking your place in the body of Christ, is so important. You, the believer, must embrace boldness in the days of adversity before us. Why? For you, believers are the natural obstacle to darkness flooding the land. You standing in your God-given authority can drive a stake in the middle of evil plans and push them out of your orbit.

Prayer, intercession, and simply doing your calling are very potent forces when taking territory in a war. Agents act as soldiers on opposing sides. One side is hostile to God and at war with Him, while the other side is enforcing, through influence, God's kingdom's desire to take place on earth. Amazingly, God loves all those who are at war with Him. He is so loving and kind and unwilling that anyone should perish, but to see His will accomplished, we must act with the Word of God in our hearts and mouths, making an influential impact everywhere our feet tread.

CHAPTER FOUR

WHERE DARKNESS REIGNS,
A REFORMER WILL RISE

And Elijah the Tishbite, of the inhabitants of Gilead, said to Ahab, "As the LORD God of Israel lives, before whom I stand, there shall not be dew nor rain these years, except at my word." ² Then the word of the LORD came to him, saying, ³ "Get away from here and turn eastward, and hide by the Brook Cherith, which flows into the Jordan. ⁴ And it will be that you shall drink from the brook, and I have commanded the ravens to feed you there." ⁵ So he went and did according to the word of the LORD, for he went and stayed by the Brook Cherith, which flows into the Jordan. ⁶ The ravens brought him bread and meat in the morning, and bread and meat in the evening; and he drank from the brook. ⁷ And it happened after a while that the brook dried up, because there had been no rain in the land.

—1 Kings 17:1-7

Darkness will push and push until it is stopped. In Ahab and Jezebel's case, they pushed evil until a supernatural reaction occurred: a reformer none of them expected stood up and began to burn their playground down.

Sowing and reaping will always cause darkness to experience a harvest of the very evil it sowed. Although it might manifest far different from expected, it will inevitably arrive with their payment. Dr. Jordan Peterson made a statement on the law of twisting the fabric of reality.

YOU CANNOT TWIST THE FABRIC OF REALITY

I've never in all my years as a clinical physiologist, and this is something that really does terrify me. I have never seen anyone ever get away with anything ever at all, even once. You know, there is that old idea that God has a book. You know, and keeps track of everything in heaven. It's like, okay, okay, you know, but maybe, it's not a book, fine. But that is a really useful thing to think about because, well, maybe you disagree. Maybe you think people get away with things all the time.

I tell you, I've never seen it. What I see instead is that thing happens right. Someone twists the fabric of reality, and they do it successfully because it doesn't snap back at them that moment. And then, like two years later, something unravels, and they get walloped, and they think, "Oh my god, that's so unfair." And then we track it, it's like, but what happened before that?...because you can't twist the fabric of reality without having it snap back! It doesn't work that way, and why would it?

I think that one of the things that really tempts people is the idea that, "Well, I can get away with it." It's like, yeah, you try, you see how well that works, it's like you get away with nothing, and that is the beginning of wisdom, and it's something that deeply terrifies me.[1]

—Dr. Jordan Peterson

Every generation eventually sees the seeds it has sown personally and as a culture come to harvest. Jezebel and Ahab sowed and pushed evil on the land to such a level that a harvest was induced. Wickedness would reap—in a way they never imagined—Elijah, the prophet of fire, arrived as a harvest of judgment against the relentless onslaught of evil sown in the land. God sent His agent, who first declared a drought in the land, and that drought was a power move by the Living God to prepare the nation for the upcoming shift to its axis of power.

In one word, with one declaration, that monumental power shift was presented on the battlefield. "As the LORD God of Israel lives, before whom I stand, there shall not be dew nor rain these years, except at my word" (1 Kings 17:1). Shortly following this moment, Elijah was led to a place of solitude to the Brook Cherith. He could drink from the brook and receive bread and meat from ravens. Elijah was provided for during the process of his mission until the time came when the brook dried up. It was a sign that his prophetic declaration had come to the apex of its purpose.

THE TIDE HAD TURNED

And it came to pass after many days that the word of the LORD came to Elijah, in the third year, saying, "Go, present yourself to Ahab, and I will send rain on the earth."

—1 Kings 18:1

Then it happened, when Ahab saw Elijah, that Ahab said to him, "Is that you, O troubler of Israel?" [18] *And he answered, "I have not troubled Israel, but you and your father's house have, in that you have forsaken the commandments of the LORD and have followed the Baals."*

—1 Kings 18:17-18

The transition began, or the turning of the tide, from when Elijah declared there would be no more rain until he said so. Power was shifting the moment he said it. The season of drought had reached a tipping point. There was a catastrophic, nation-crushing issue affecting everyone and everything. No one was exempt. That is why they listened; the nation was primed to hear a reformer.

WHEN A MAN LIVES FOR NOTHING, HE WILL SERVE THE HIGHEST BIDDER

Ahab couldn't understand why Elijah was so against him. "Is that you, my enemy?" Yet, we do see Ahab's civility toward Elijah. When a man lives for nothing, he will serve the highest bidder—in Ahab's case, situational ethics and morals—whichever gave him what he desired. Ahab was enslaved, wearing a crown, and at his own doing.

Ahab was likely the sort who would quote the exploits of his fathers before him, telling the tales of his abilities. I envision him as a pampered aristocrat adept at winning people over with his charm at a social gathering. He would cozy up to whoever seemed most beneficial, play the role of a good guy, and talk big about life to validate himself to those around him. But he would whine and sulk to Jezebel when he couldn't get what he wanted, such as in Naboth's vineyard (1 Kings 21:1-16).

Ahab's cowardice was that he ran to Jezebel with his complaints, and the vile woman would get him what he wanted, not for his satisfaction, but her own. She wanted power, and by bringing the king something he felt helpless to attain, she would step in with her cauterized emotions, showing zero remorse or empathy, and achieve what was desired by any means necessary.

Jezebel was never one to blush. Something is unsettling about that kind of person. They are shameless in all the wrong ways, incapable of humility, and only able to see what they desire.

But now, with the arrival of God's prophet, His reformer, all of Ahab's maneuvering and alliances would not help him in this time of extreme desperation. God had taken all their leverage away; now, it was Elijah's turn.

ELIJAH CAME TO DESTROY THE WORKS OF EVIL

Elijah had an assignment to destroy Jezebel's work and bring rain to the land. Spiritually speaking, God has each generation equipped with reformers who will usher in this supernatural force marshaled by heaven to stop a wave of evil that would come to wash over the generation they live in. The prophet Elijah was a source of immense frustration for the evil duo. Nothing they tried seemed to work against him except the threat Jezebel issued, which caused Elijah to run to the wilderness. Still, nothing they attempted ever could stop Elijah when he was on point.

Each generation is in desperate need of a reformer who will push back the powers of darkness and show the culture there is a God in heaven.

> *Who gave Himself for our sins, that He might deliver us from this present evil age, according to the will of our God and Father.*
>
> **—Galatians 1:4**

Galatians 1:4 is a very comforting scripture regarding Jesus, who gave Himself for our sins that He might deliver us for this present evil age. What makes this scripture so powerful is that after it states that Jesus gave Himself to deliver us from this present evil age, the astonishing truth is that *it is God's will!* That's right! It is God's will that you be delivered from this present evil age.

We are at the brink of something monumental that has not been seen or heard recently—the way-maker anointing is rising, filled with repentance, restoration, and breathtaking, miraculous responses to the wicked Antichrist regime. The forerunner anointing to prepare the way will once again demonstrate to the land that the spirit of Elijah is here!

At the forefront of this narrative is the spirit of Jezebel!

Reclaiming a hijacked generation that has been run off the rails from a coordinated and marshaled assault socially, politically, financially, and even genetically is not a small task. Standing on the highway marked the broad path of destruction, and crying out and rescuing as many as possible was not difficult. In today's world, society is making it nearly impossible! Ancient spirits are permitted by leaders abroad who are so blinded that it's as if they wish to host these nefarious entities set out to capture and destroy this generation—as they do in each cycle of history.

THERE IS NOTHING NEW UNDER THE SUN

Is there anything of which it may be said, "See, this is new"? It has already been in ancient times before us. [11] *There is no remembrance of former things, nor will there be any remembrance of things that are to come by those who will come after.*

—Ecclesiastes 1:10-11

Encouraging might not be the word some would use, but there is an argument to be made when looking at the turbulence we face: There is nothing new under the sun! Yes, it is true. Cycles of history repeat themselves, and knowing this brings peace. If one generation faced unbelievable atrocities only to survive them and bring forth another generation to follow them, then we have hope for our future as well.

Only a limited number of these cycles will occur before the end of this age, and they will increase with intensity until the end arrives. Before the end can fully come, the pressure of the kingdom of God wanting to manifest will induce power-filled voices and believers who will stand in power and authority, unlike any time in our history. If you are reading this, then it is you to whom this is referencing. You were born for the days we are in right now. It doesn't matter your age or station in life. All that matters is answering the high call of the great God of heaven. Your yes is all He needs; keep giving it to Him, and you will see the goodness of the Lord in the land of the living (Psalm 27:13).

THE END OF THE AGE WAS INEVITABLE FROM THE ORIGINAL REBELLION

And war broke out in heaven: Michael and his angels fought with the dragon; and the dragon and his angels fought, 8 but they did not prevail, nor was a place found for them in heaven any longer. 9 So the great dragon was cast out, that serpent of old, called the Devil and Satan, who deceives the whole world; he was cast to the earth, and his angels were cast out with him.

—Revelation 12:7-9

Civilizations have risen and declined, all under the influence of an age's old cosmic hostility. This ruptured the order of God's plan for man from the beginning. This continuous and long conflict very much operates how a cold war does—though it is not truly a cold war, it is hot in all actuality, only cloaked with the shroud known as the natural world. Most in the natural world are in the clutches of the dark forces waging the conflict against godliness. The cultural beachhead for this war intersects in the hearts and minds of each generation. This is deceptively a cold war mainly because it operates with a normalcy bias that lulls those affected by its spell into an unconcerned state, even as the world sinks slowly into the dark mire of depravity.

BREAKING A MIND-BLINDING SPIRIT

But even if our gospel is veiled, it is veiled to those who are perishing, 4 whose minds the god of this age has blinded, who do not believe, lest the light of the gospel of the glory of Christ, who is the image of God, should shine on them.

—2 Corinthians 4:3-4

It is only becoming increasingly urgent that we recognize the signs of the times, as we are indeed in the last of the last days. In these times, a generation with little exposure to the One True Living God risks falling prey to their self-centeredness. They are vulnerable to the deceptive agendas of evil, which hide behind the facade of cultural relevance and the distortion of truth. This is the work of the demonic hordes enforcing the spirit of the age, much like Jezebel, who demanded her land conform to her sick and perverse way of ruling. Our modern culture is all too familiar with the effects of this *alternative to truth* lifestyle. The mind-blinding of a generation is leading them away from the knowledge of God.

Even now, the cold/hot war is here; it is confronting you right now—it has been this way since Adam left the garden. Warfare is not only directed at you, but it is widespread against the entire culture you are living in. Although it may seem like a cold war, let me assure you, it is a very hot war! Weapons are being implemented in this collision daily and from each side of the conflict. You possess a secret weapon given to you by God Himself from the beginning. After all, we see the darkness rising and rising, but God would never leave the world without light or hope; He would never allow society to operate under the complete dominance of evil without offering weapons and mechanisms to respond and fight back—in the case of evil clawing for global territory He, the great God of heaven, has a secret weapon available to you! Something as if it were up His sleeve to spring on the world as a counteraction against wickedness.

GOD'S SECRET WEAPON

Do you know the ultimate weapon God has for these last days? His first and last line of defense and offense in this world? It is you! He doesn't have anyone else but those like you who are part of the body of Christ. You are the secret weapon, and being part of the body of Christ in the correct position in the right lane will cause the body to function at its highest potential.

You possess a tremendous God-given weapon. Something the devil and his fallen hordes are envious of, a power that trumps the influence of spiritual beings—you have your body and free will. I call this "free moral agency."

It's not just an earth suit you have. It's a powerful tool. You have the power to choose what you will do with it. The battle lines are drawn, but darkness desperately wants it to camouflage so that it might influence you for its dark agenda. This makes the battleground in your mind and choices even more crucial. Your mind is the *territory*; both God and the devil are territorial—what will you do?

Questioning the actions of everyone alive is productive, but the ultimate effectiveness for any generation is to give their territory over to the One True Living God. His cry to the world through His preachers is "repent and be saved!" His cry to the saved is, "Renew your mind!" God is territorial and, as a Spirit, can only operate according to the laws He created. Jesus' sacrifice was massive; it was everything. He destroyed the kingdom of darkness in one action, yet free moral agents known as humankind are left in the balance. What is required with the cascading darkness and the perilous times of evil we are experiencing? How do we see victory? How do we warn a culture that will not hear?

SPECIAL ANOINTING FOR YOUR GENERATION

A special anointing is required! Every generation has experienced one type of evil or another—the greater the deception, the greater the anointing sent by God.

In the case of Noah, he warned everyone of what was to come and was obedient to the Lord in his generation. Just imagine all the insults and jokes that must have been told at Noah's expense. That is, of course, until the day heaven opened, as did the deep! This resulted in a global cataclysm of such immense scale, unlike anything experienced in recorded biblical history, that it exploded onto the scene with awe-inspiring power.

> *By faith Noah, being divinely warned of things not yet seen, moved with godly fear, prepared an ark for the saving of his household, by which he condemned the world and became heir of the righteousness which is according to faith.*
>
> **—Hebrews 11:7**

And did not spare the ancient world, but saved Noah, one of eight people, a preacher of righteousness, bringing in the flood on the world of the ungodly.

—**2 Peter 2:5**

Noah was a preacher of righteousness. He was a standard for his generation, speaking out and preaching righteousness to a perverse generation.

SOME THINGS THAT HARDEN THE HEARTS OF A CULTURE

When a reformer steps into a culture hardened to the things of God, it is often the result of several things:

- Wicked rulers
- False religions
- Crisis fatigue: One horrible event after another
- Poverty through famine
- Disillusionment by a powerless representation of God

The display of power is crucial to counter a culture suffering from hardness of heart. Arguments and persuasions, while correct, are not complete without the backing of power. When a culture has strayed, a powerful demonstration will serve as a potent reminder of its values and beliefs, declaring who God is.

This is why it is of utmost importance that every generation receives a wake-up call.

SIGNS OF A CULTURE SET FREE

In the wake of a reformer comes a culture set free—or at least the tools and opportunity of a culture to walk into the future with an illuminated perspective. No other example of this will exceed the last great reformation than the *Millennial Reign of Jesus Christ* after His return and victory over the beast and false prophet at the Battle of Armageddon. The Lord Jesus will rule for one thousand years on earth and, during that time, will allow humanity to know Him and witness His reign. Talk about the opportunity to walk into a future with an illuminated perspective!

Regardless of how good or bad one season is, we know that history has shown us patterns that repeat throughout the arc of societies, which rise and fall. Simplifying this point is the famous quote that references different times:

> "Hard times create strong men, strong men create good times, good times create weak men, and weak men create hard times."

> **—G. Michael Hopf**

Something that can be certain is that reformers, agents of change, or those who work for God in their generation will always leave the world a better place than how they discovered it. The following is a list showing signs of a generation impacted by the presence of a reformer:

+ Righteous rulers
+ Reformers confronting duplicity
+ Demonstration of God's power
+ Experiencing biblical prosperity
+ Blinders removed to the goodness of God

RIGHTEOUS RULERS

*When the righteous are in authority, the people rejoice;
but when a wicked man rules, the people groan.*

—Proverbs 29:2

Proverbs 29:2 is self-explanatory. When the wicked man rules, the people groan. One of the responsibilities of the body of Christ is to make a kingdom impact everywhere they are, even in the highest offices in the land. The devil will happily fill whatever we vacate and leave a void of our influence. On the other hand, when the righteous are in a place of authority, the people rejoice! Which is the result of good things happening to them and their land.

REFORMERS CONFRONT DUPLICITY

Nothing speaks to this more clearly than Elijah asking, "How long will you falter between two opinions?" Reformers not only make the statement, but they also come with a demonstration of power. This is what Elijah did—he was God's agent to bring the fire!

DEMONSTRATION OF GOD'S POWER

Of all the ones who offered a demonstration of God's power, Moses is one of the top characters. He did so amid a wicked kingdom. God used Moses, the reformer prophet, to rescue His people from tyranny. Signs, wonders, and profound miracles were performed to execute God's will for His people to be delivered. Our greatest example of all is Jesus! Consider what He did in front of the Pharisees and Sadducees. Miracles upon miracles, and at times, offensive miracles! One example is when Jesus healed on the Sabbath—a direct offense to the Pharisees' interpretation of the law.

> *And He entered the synagogue again, and a man was there who had a withered hand. ² So they watched Him closely, whether He would heal him on the Sabbath, so that they might accuse Him. ³ And He said to the man who had the withered hand, "Step forward." ⁴ Then He said to them, "Is it lawful on the Sabbath to do good or to do evil, to save life or to kill?" But they kept silent.* ⁵ *And **when He had looked around at them with anger, being grieved by the hardness of their hearts, He said to the man, "Stretch out your hand." And he stretched it out, and his hand was restored as whole as the other.*** ⁶ *Then the Pharisees went out and immediately plotted with the Herodians against Him, how they might destroy Him.*
>
> **—Mark 3:1-6**

Jesus was angry at their hardness of heart and responded with an irrefutable miracle to come against their arguments. Among the many significant reasons Jesus did this was that He was doing what reformers do—reforming the current ingrained and hardened institutionalism to breathe life back into it.

EXPERIENCING BIBLICAL PROSPERITY

> *"And all nations will call you blessed, for you will be a delightful land," says the Lord of hosts.*
>
> **—Malachi 3:12**

The word "delightful" implies your land and life will continue to increase, a breakthrough and overflow to the pleasure of God. One definition of "delight" is that it is a more permanent pleasure than joy. Delight is God using your life to shine and break the influence of darkness over nations. There will be a battle, but stand firm. If you do not faint, there is a reward at the end of the day. This is part of biblical prosperity, which is something reformers bring to the land!

> A good man leaves an inheritance to his children's children, but the wealth of the sinner is stored up for the righteous.
>
> **—Proverbs 13:22**

> I will give you the treasures of darkness and hidden riches of secret places, that you may know that I, the Lord, who call you by your name, Am the God of Israel.
>
> **—Isaiah 45:3**

Ultimately, biblical prosperity results from enforcing God's principles in any culture.

BLINDERS REMOVED TO THE GOODNESS OF GOD

> But even if our gospel is veiled, it is veiled to those who are perishing, ⁴ whose minds the god of this age has blinded, who do not believe, lest the light of the gospel of the glory of Christ, who is the image of God, should shine on them.
>
> **—2 Corinthians 4:3-4**

Sadly, most will go through life having never experienced the goodness of God—The One, True, and Living God who loves them unconditionally and longs to have a relationship with them. Unfortunately, the god of this age has hindered so many from knowing who God is. Consequently, this is why we must preach the gospel to everyone. It is the prescribed way to remove the blinders and expose the hearers to the goodness of God.

> *For since, in the wisdom of God, the world through wisdom did not know God, it pleased God through the foolishness of the message preached to save those who believe.*
>
> **—1 Corinthians 1:21**

Even though there are blinders on many people, and if the gospel we preach bounces off them, we are to continue preaching, for how will they hear if we quit?

> *How then shall they call on Him in whom they have not believed? And how shall they believe in Him of whom they have not heard? And how shall they hear without a preacher?*
>
> **—Romans 10:14**

PROPHETS AND REFORMERS BREAK UP THE HARDNESS OF HEARTS

> *For thus says the LORD to the men of Judah and Jerusalem: "Break up your fallow ground, and do not sow among thorns."*
>
> **—Jeremiah 4:3**

Sow for yourselves righteousness; reap in mercy; break up your fallow ground, for it is time to seek the LORD, till He comes and rains righteousness on you.

—Hosea 10:12

"Fallow ground" means *a crusted-over, hard ground that must be broken up with a plow.* That is what the voice of a prophet or reformer does in a generation. They bust through the topsoil that has become hardened, and due to no use or leaving the ground dormant, it encrusts the hearts of people who become unable to hear.

THE LAST OF THE LAST DAYS

For 2,000 years, society has been in what the Bible calls the "last days." We are currently in the last of the last days and approaching the "end times." This period will determine how we will enter the coming phase—the End Times, including the Millennial Reign of Jesus and eternity future.

Therefore, since all these things will be dissolved, what manner of persons ought you to be in holy conduct and godliness, ¹² looking for and hastening the coming of the day of God, because of which the heavens will be dissolved, being on fire, and the elements will melt with fervent heat?

—2 Peter 3:11-12

Our walk as a dedicated believer should reflect those who carry an expectation for the coming of the Lord. Each believer should count themselves as one who answers the statement in 2 Peter 3:11, "What manner of persons ought you to be in holy conduct and godliness." A true believer will respond with a life of dedication to Jesus Christ. It is, however, vital that we understand our behavior and walk of obedience unto the high calling God has given each of us—a hand on the wheel. I am referring to the timeline for when the Lord will return.

THE COMING GREAT AND TERRIBLE DAY OF THE LORD

Once again, volcanic pressure is building, and a radical shift in society has been unleashed, leading to malice and deception beyond all reason and logic. Global society is being conditioned to bow the knee to all things antichrist in nature as the Lord's return draws near. In the end, when Jesus returns, it will be a great and terrible day that is not tolerable for any living person.

> ...for the day of the LORD is great and very terrible; who can endure it?
>
> —Joel 2:11

Along this journey toward what the Bible calls *the great and terrible day of the Lord* is the placement of agents of clarity. They are set apart—called out from among the culture to speak the uncompromising truth while carrying out a generational assignment. How these are responded to and treated will determine much of the outcome for that generation. Let us consider the two prophets in Revelation, the angels in Sodom, the prophets Jeremiah and Noah, and all the voices and prophets who stood up as a voice crying out in their generation. Also, consider the responses to these.

> For the great day of His wrath has come, and who is able to stand?
>
> **—Revelation 6:17**

When considering historical cycles or dispensations, it appears that often, the Lord has voices in place warning, preparing, and even guiding on the cusp or even while amid such events.

LAST-DAYS CULTURE

Today, crimes against humanity are celebrated and polished away through verbiage marshaled for one purpose: pure brainwashing of our children. Why? To build an army of non-thinking, order-taking, Antichrist soldiers committed to a false ideology filled with self-harm, mutilation, perverse identity, and a complete abandonment of all that is good and virtuous.

It is this tsunami that appears from generation to generation. Growing with a veracious intensity that the passing of time will only outdo the last evil unless it is stopped or exposed. Nothing will stand in its way and certainly will not recover in its wake! Regardless of this impossibility, the imperative realization must awaken. A clarity, a fire of rebellion against the rejoicing of sickness, a figure standing firmly in the middle of evil's freeway and declaring, "No more! Your evil reign of tyranny will come to an end! Your vile system will fall, for I stand fearlessly against you, not in my strength, but in the strength of the One who sent me. Of whom I represent and of whom I belong." Yet, within this prophetic narrative comes the placement of influence and the idea an eruption is coming. Pressure is building toward it every day!

REFORMERS—THE ANTIDOTE TO A CULTURE GONE MAD

Reformers speak and act in such ways that they begin as a fly in the ointment, like an annoyance, an irritation to these high and mighty arrogant fools. Sometimes, the Lord raises up a minority to go against the violent rapids when He finds a free moral agent completely surrendered with discipline and tenacity, walking in practiced holiness, and living in marked obedience to the service of the Lord.

Whatever the institution cannot control, it must kill or persecute.

Every generation faces evil, which may seem new, but nothing is new under the sun. Any form of wickedness that emerges is a repackaged version of an ancient foe. And in each generation, the answer rises to meet evil and stop it. Reformers often emerge, carrying a non-conformist spirit, as an assigned entity for disrupting the wicked and reconciliation for the innocent. The cycles of time and seasons repeat the rise of both influences and will continue. Dark spiritual forces always give way, or at least are designed to serve the agenda of the Antichrist.

NO, YOU MOVE!

A stupor of deception always seems to accompany them, yet only one thing comes to interrupt these demonic players. Like a stake offensively driven by these wicked agencies and ideologues, the spirit of Elijah stands. Alone or with a fellowship, this assigned generational spirit of truth will always tell the evil, wicked forces, "No, you move!"

Like a scene in a film or the hero in a story, the spirit of Elijah carries the heart of God, which states that God can save by many, by few, or even by one.

WRECKING BALL OR RECONCILER

Whether one becomes a wrecking ball or a reconciler is not a matter of chance but a result of the culture's behavior and zeitgeist. The spirit of Elijah stands for change, and our collective responsibility is to usher in the kingdom of God.

John the Baptist preached repentance, speaking out shamelessly against the political filth of his time, yet his highest calling was to prepare the way for the Messiah.

The Spirit of the Lord spoke to me one day as I prayed about America's future. Out of great concern, I asked the Lord, "Is America going down? Is it all over?" The response was sudden and direct from the Lord. "No," He said, "America has one more round...the young lions are coming!" Reformers who are fearless and filled with cause.

PUNISH THE DARKNESS

*Let the high praises of God be in their mouth, and a two-edged sword in their hand, 7 to execute vengeance on the nations, and punishment on the peoples; 8 **to bind their kings with chains, and their nobles with fetters of iron;** 9 to execute on them the written judgment—This is an honor for all His godly ones. Praise the LORD!*

—Psalm 149:6-9

There is a level of warfare that releases punishment on darkness. Psalm 149 says, "...bind their kings with chains, and their nobles with fetters of iron." Spiritual violence weaponized and marshaled to punish disobedience is different from pushing back the darkness.

For though we walk in the flesh, we do not war according to the flesh, 4 for the weapons of our warfare are not of the flesh, but divinely powerful for the destruction of fortresses. 5 We are destroying speculations and every lofty thing raised up against the knowledge of God, and we are taking every thought captive to the obedience of Christ,

^{6} *and we are ready to punish all disobedience, whenever your obedience is complete.*

—2 Corinthians 10:3-6 NASB1995

DIAMOND SEEDS SOWN UNDER INTENSE PRESSURE PRODUCING THE FINEST VALUE

You must know that the Lord sees all your days and sacrifices, much like Cornelius, whose alms and offerings came before the Lord. Everyone who chooses to honor God, no matter the time or season, will be honored by the Great God of heaven.

Diamond seeds are the actions of those who have stood with character, sown with pain and tears, regardless of what the outcome looked like to them. Psalm 126:5 defines this understanding: "Those who sow in tears shall reap in joy." That sowing of tears or when you did what was right before the Lord repeatedly until it produced a form of diamonds—precious gems, or symbolically an outcome with tremendous value.

Those who stand in obedience and faithfulness will rise to their highest potential. God is saving the best for last; I declare that it is you. Regardless of what you have done, where you have failed, or anything else that would tell you you're disqualified, you can start immediately and step into all God has for you. God is so good that He can make plans B, C, and D so good that they outdo plan A!

You are fully equipped to join this last day's narrative, to produce diamond seeds, and to rise against darkness.

CHAPTER FIVE

THE SPIRIT OF ELIJAH
ONCE AND AGAIN

And so it was, when they had crossed over, that Elijah said to Elisha, "Ask! What may I do for you, before I am taken away from you?" Elisha said, "Please let a double portion of your spirit be upon me."

—2 Kings 2:9

Now when the sons of the prophets who were from Jericho saw him, they said, "The spirit of Elijah rests on Elisha." And they came to meet him, and bowed to the ground before him.

—2 Kings 2:15

DEFINING THE SPIRIT OF ELIJAH

The spirit of Elijah is defined as standing against the oppression of an evil regime while operating in generational cooperation. This narrative of generational cooperation is not limited to a single era. Still, it spans across generations, seeing the will of God and His people come to pass in a multigenerational capacity. It's a larger, enduring narrative that we, as believers, are part of.

When we consider all the scripture references regarding the spirit of Elijah, it becomes clear that this term, often used in pop culture Christianity, has a deeper significance. My purpose for using the phrase "spirit of Elijah" is to define the familiar conflict of national and even global powers that seek to usurp the authority given by God for the good of humanity. It's about activating those who would rise with a word from God to oppose such forces.

As a prophet, Elijah was not only tasked with enforcing God's will in his generation but also with passing on a generational anointing. This act of empowerment, symbolized by the transfer of his mantle to Elisha, ensured that the spirit of Elijah would continue to influence and guide future generations.

GENERATIONAL EMPOWERMENT

It shall be that whoever escapes the sword of Hazael, Jehu will kill; and whoever escapes the sword of Jehu, Elisha will kill.

—1 Kings 19:17

Elijah didn't finish all his assignments, but Elisha and Jehu did. Again, this drives the understanding that Elijah released a generational mantle. What is interesting and even humorous is that Elijah seemed not to care who did what after him. He was moody and depressed at times but clear and powerful when the word of the Lord came to him.

In contrast, Elisha was more focused and far less up and down, at least according to scripture. Although he did get angry, he was very much on point with what God called him to do.

DOUBLE PORTION

When Elisha asked for a double portion, he was not asking for twice as much as Elijah had, but twice as much as any other successor would receive, which is the standard inheritance right of the firstborn, who would "carry the torch" for the family. Elisha requests that he receive the status of the principal successor to Elijah (2 Kings 2:9).[1]

When it comes to the terminology "double portion," there might be a supernatural voltage attached to his being that radiated like electricity from him, as in a man coming back to life after being thrown onto the bones of Elijah—beyond Elijah's bones bringing a man back to life, the Bible doesn't clearly define a radiance or electrical force of a double portion on Elisha. What is said is that the sons of the prophets, or the prophets-in-training who were part of the school of the prophets, recognized that Elisha had upon him the spirit of Elijah. How did they know this? Was it because Elisha's face glowed like Moses' after coming down from the mountain? No, not at all, at least based on what we read. They recognized that Elijah's works rested upon Elisha, not to mention that Elisha also had his mantle on himself.

FIFTY WITNESSES TO ELISHA RECEIVING THE SPIRIT OF ELIJAH

And fifty men of the sons of the prophets went and stood facing them at a distance, while the two of them stood by the Jordan.

—2 Kings 2:7

At least fifty men from the school of the prophets witnessed Elijah's translation, the first miracle involving Elisha, followed by his dividing the waters of the Jordan River with his mantle. These 50 testified that the *spirit of Elijah* now rested upon Elisha. He was, therefore, immediately accepted as the successor of the translated prophet, as indicated by their bowing before him—2 Kings 2:15, "Now when the sons of the prophets who were from Jericho saw him, they said, 'The spirit of Elijah rests on Elisha.' And they came to meet him, and bowed to the ground before him."²

WHO WERE THE SONS OF THE PROPHETS—WHAT WAS THE SCHOOL OF THE PROPHETS?

Now the sons of the prophets who were at Bethel came out to Elisha, and said to him, "Do you know that the LORD will take away your master from over you today?" And he said, "Yes, I know; keep silent!" ⁴ Then Elijah said to him, "Elisha, stay here, please, for the LORD has sent me on to Jericho." But he said, "As the LORD lives, and as your soul lives, I will not leave you!" So they came to Jericho. ⁵ Now the sons of the prophets who were at Jericho came to Elisha and said to him, "Do you know that the LORD will take away your master from over you today?" So he answered, "Yes, I know; keep silent!"

—2 Kings 2:3-5

Here, we see the "the sons of the prophets" and Elijah, but independent revelations were made to the two "schools" at Bethel and Jericho. Without knowledge from the other, both schools came out to tell Elisha what would happen that day with Elijah being taken. This action is humorous as it is such a prophetic trait! Prophetic people want to be the first to tell you what they "know" by the spirit. Among the many possibilities, these locations must have been where they practiced hearing what the Lord was saying by getting in tune with His Voice. What is very interesting is that this was pre–Holy Spirit baptism. Thus, it is reasonable to consider that sons of the prophets were likely those who had a gift in their person from birth, and once recognized, they would need to be trained to hear God directly.

Some commentators suggest that these prophets were the divine philosophers, instructors, and guides of the Hebrews in piety and virtue. This would show that prophetic people go beyond simply hearing God and saying what they hear, which is a correct but incomplete understanding. These sons of the prophets generally lived in solitude, being seen in public mainly when they had to deliver some message from God. Their lifestyle and dwellings were plain, simple, and consistent.

PUPILS OF THE PROPHETS

Sons of the prophets were pupils of the prophets who were trained in religious and spiritual matters. They were not a monastic order but a group of theological students studying the law and the history of God's people, along with sacred poetry and music. There were several schools of the prophets from the days of Samuel to the New Testament times when Israel was a nation.

> *After that you shall come to the hill of God where the Philistine garrison is. And it will happen, when you have come there to the city, that you will meet **a group of prophets** coming down from the high place with a stringed instrument, a tambourine, a flute, and a harp before them; and they will be prophesying.*
>
> **—1 Samuel 10:5**

Then Saul sent messengers to take David. And when they saw the group of prophets prophesying, and Samuel standing as leader over them, the Spirit of God came upon the messengers of Saul, and they also prophesied.

—1 Samuel 19:20

ELIJAH WAS HEADMASTER OF SEVERAL SCHOOLS

Gilgal

*And Elisha returned to **Gilgal,** and there was a famine in the land. Now the sons of the prophets were sitting before him; and he said to his servant, "Put on the large pot, and boil stew for the sons of the prophets."*

—2 Kings 4:38

Bethel

Bethel is where Jeroboam had his altar and one of his golden calves.

Now the sons of the prophets who were at Bethel came out to Elisha…

—2 Kings 2:3

Jericho and Other Places

Now the sons of the prophets who were at Jericho came to Elisha and said to him....

—2 Kings 2:5

Now when the sons of the prophets who were from Jericho saw him, they said....

—2 Kings 2:15

ELISHA SUCCEEDED ELIJAH

Elisha succeeded Elijah over these schools of the prophets, also known as the sons of the prophets, and Elisha even enlarged them.

And the sons of the prophets said to Elisha, "See now, the place where we dwell with you is too small for us. ² Please, let us go to the Jordan, and let every man take a beam from there, and let us make there a place where we may dwell." So he answered, "Go."

—2 Kings 6:1-2

*And Elisha returned to Gilgal, and there was a famine in the land. Now the **sons of the prophets** were sitting before him; and he said to his servant, "Put on the large pot, and boil stew for the **sons of the prophets.**"*

—2 Kings 4:38

And he said, "All is well. My master has sent me, saying, 'Indeed, just now two young men of the sons of the prophets have come to me from the mountain of Ephraim. Please give them a talent of silver and two changes of garments.'"

—2 Kings 5:22

And Elisha the prophet called one of the sons of the prophets, and said to him, "Get yourself ready, take this flask of oil in your hand, and go to Ramoth Gilead."

—2 Kings 9:1

Twice, Elisha testified that he knew Elijah was to be translated that day, and that day, Elijah was taken away (2 Kings 2:3, 2 Kings 2:5). This revelation may have come through prophets other than Elijah. Still, Elijah knew it, too, for he was translated by faith, similar to Enoch (Hebrews 11:5).

On both occasions, Elisha steadfastly dismissed the prophetic students who were eagerly informing him of Elijah's impending departure. It is intriguing to note that these two schools of prophets had a revelation of the event, indicating their keen insight into such scenarios. Despite the students' revelatory moments, Elisha's unwavering focus and determination to stay on his mission is truly inspiring.[3]

ELIJAH REPRESENTS PREPARATION, REFORMATION, AND GENERATIONAL IMPARTATION!

The phrase "spirit of Elijah" represents all Elijah did and the type of influence, mentality, and operation he introduced to the culture he lived in. The same applies to anyone who will rise to meet the purpose of God in their time. This means you! You have everything you need in Jesus to walk boldly and push back against the onslaught of darkness. Maybe this means through prayer, through your appointed job, or a ministry you are called to start. It represents any area of life where you are planted as salt and light with the direct intention to make a massive impact by the Spirit of the Lord.

WE SEE ELIJAH DOING SEVERAL THINGS:

+ Elijah prophesied that it would not rain.
+ Elijah returned to confront evil, reminding the people that the God who answered by fire is the One True Living God.
+ Elijah mentored Elisha as a son in the prophetic.
+ Elijah had schools of the prophets. He trained and set up locations for equipping.
+ Elijah empowered Elisha and Jehu to carry his mandate to the next generation.

THE SPIRIT OF ELIJAH WAS ON JOHN THE BAPTIST TO PREPARE AND DECLARE THE WAY OF THE LORD!

As they departed, Jesus began to say to the multitudes concerning John: "What did you go out into the wilderness to see? A reed shaken by the wind? 8 But what did you go out to see? A man clothed in soft garments? Indeed, those who wear soft clothing are in kings' houses. 9 But what did you go out to see? A prophet? Yes, I say to you, and more than a prophet. [10] *For this is he of whom it is written:* **'Behold, I send My messenger before Your face, who will prepare Your way before You.'** [11] *"Assuredly, I say to you, among those born of women there has not risen one greater than John the Baptist; but he who is least in the kingdom of heaven is greater than he.* [12] *And from the days of John the Baptist until now the kingdom of heaven suffers violence, and the violent take it by force.* [13] *For all the prophets and the law prophesied until John.* [14] *And if you are willing to receive it, he is Elijah who is to come.* [15] *He who has ears to hear, let him hear!"*

—**Matthew 11:7-15**

John the Baptist was a forerunner to Jesus. He was to prepare the way and restore all things by coming before Jesus to preach, prophesy, denounce sin, call the nation to repentance, and even hold the leaders to account. Ultimately, this led to part one: restoring all things.

FORERUNNER TO PART ONE AND THE UPCOMING SEQUEL!

Assuredly, I say to you, among those born of women there has not risen one greater than John the Baptist; but he who is least in the kingdom of heaven is greater than he.

—**Matthew 11:11**

Part one refers to the first time Jesus came. The second time, Jesus' arrival will open the next chapter leading up to the finale of the restoration of all things. If there was an announcement the first time by a forerunner, that same spirit of Elijah may very well come upon the body of Christ to announce the return of Jesus the second time.

Why? Because the least in the New Testament is greater than the greatest prophet of the Old Testament. John the Baptist was the greatest prophet due to the responsibility and honor of preparing the way and announcing Jesus. After Jesus' death and resurrection, we are under His blood and a New Covenant on better promises. Those under this New Covenant are greater than John the Baptist because they are renewed, born again, and connected in the Spirit to God the Father because of Christ Jesus the Son.

JOHN THE BAPTIST PREPARED AND DECLARED THE WAY OF THE LORD

As a forerunner to Jesus' first appearance, John prepared the way as a mouthpiece, even in baptizing Jesus. In the beginning, he declared who Jesus was: "Behold the Lamb of God, who takes away the sin of the world" (John 1:29). Restoring all things was set in motion by John declaring and preparing the way for Jesus to arrive and announcing Him when He came into focus. John famously stated, "He must increase, I must decrease…" (John 3:30). This is also what the spirit of Elijah does—prepares the way, then steps aside out of the way.

Much like Elijah, who ascended in a whirlwind but left his mantle for Elisha, Elijah's role was not just in his own time. He prepared the way for his successors, ensuring the continuity of the divine plan through training, impartation, and instructions.

> *And His disciples asked Him, saying, "Why then do the scribes say that Elijah must come first?"* [11] *Jesus answered and said to them, "Indeed, Elijah is coming first and will restore all things.* [12] *But I say to you that Elijah has come*

already, and they did not know him but did to him what-
ever they wished. Likewise, the Son of Man is also about
*to suffer at their hands." * [13] *Then the disciples understood*
that He spoke to them of John the Baptist.

—Matthew 17:10-13

And they asked Him, saying, "Why do the scribes say
*that Elijah must come first?" * [12] *Then He answered and*
told them, "Indeed, Elijah is coming first and restores all
things. And how is it written concerning the Son of Man,
that He must suffer many things and be treated with con-
tempt? [13] *But I say to you that Elijah has also come, and*
they did to him whatever they wished, as it is written of
him."

—Mark 9:11-13

SPIRIT OF ELIJAH BEFORE THE GREAT TRIBULATION

Behold, I will send you Elijah the prophet before the com-
ing of the great and dreadful day of the LORD. [6] *And*
he will turn the hearts of the fathers to the children, and
the hearts of the children to their fathers, lest I come and
strike the earth with a curse.

—Malachi 4:5-6

Malachi 4:5-6 was a prophetic word regarding one who was to
come, John the Baptist, an absolute reformer in his day, but the comparison is to the prophet Elijah.

What about Elijah made him a point of reference for a coming day and would be fulfilled by John the Baptist? Saying, "I will send you Elijah the prophet before the coming of the great and dreadful day of the Lord," is a high point of interest, as most would have missed that John the Baptist fulfilled this prophecy. If Jesus had not pointed it out directly, it would have largely remained an abstract prophecy to the people of his day. Jesus had to point out that John the Baptist was Elijah, who was to come.

JOHN THE BAPTIST'S RESPONSE WHEN ASKED IF HE WAS ELIJAH

And they asked him, "What then? Are you Elijah?" He said, "I am not." "Are you the Prophet?" And he answered, "No." 22 *Then they said to him, "Who are you, that we may give an answer to those who sent us? What do you say about yourself?"* 23 *He said: "I am 'The voice of one crying in the wilderness: "Make straight the way of the Lord,"' as the prophet Isaiah said."*

—John 1:21-23

Spoken like a true prophet—filled with humility and saw himself as less, not more.

Did John know he was the Elijah who was to come? I think he most likely had an inclination that something special was happening in his time, from jumping in Elizabeth's womb to coming into proximity to Jesus. Later, he prophesied Jesus was *the Lamb of God who would take away the sin of the world.* Additionally, John heard the Voice of God saying, "This is my beloved Son in whom I AM well pleased..." (Matthew 3:17).

John also burned for what was right in the land—just like Elijah. Yet, despite all those things, John's response was never one of self-exaltation in any way. He knew his role and grace, which qualified him even more to walk in the spirit of Elijah.

LIKE ELIJAH, JOHN THE BAPTIST GOT DISCOURAGED

Another aspect of John's personality is that he gets discouraged, just like Elijah. After confronting Herod and Herodias, he was imprisoned. During that time, John sent messengers to Jesus, asking if He was the one or if they should look for another! That is quite a statement after the audible Voice of God had already told him who Jesus was—His beloved Son.

> And when John had heard in prison about the works of Christ, he sent two of his disciples [3] and said to Him, "Are You the Coming One, or do we look for another?" [4] Jesus answered and said to them, "Go and tell John the things which you hear and see: [5] The blind see and the lame walk; the lepers are cleansed and the deaf hear; the dead are raised up and the poor have the gospel preached to them. [6] And blessed is he who is not offended because of Me."
>
> —Matthew 11:2-6

Notice Jesus said, "And blessed is he who is not offended because of Me." This is similar to Elijah's behavior when he ran from Jezebel, saying, "I am the only one left." But the Lord God reminded Elijah of the seven thousand who had not bowed their knees to Baal. (See 1 Kings 19:18.)

ELIJAH AND KING HEROD

Just as Elijah appeared on the scene in the Book of Kings like a bolt of lightning to the dark powers that ruled the land, John the Baptist confronted Herod and Herodias about their immoral relationship.

God used Elijah as a prophet to shake Jezebel's domineering control. Following in his fiery footsteps was John the Baptist, a contemporary of Jesus, who bore witness to Jesus while directly confronting Herod and Herodias.

For the sake of comparison, and considering that Jesus called John "Elijah, who was to come," it is not a far leap to recognize the traits of Elijah in John the Baptist's life, especially in his bold confrontation of Herod and Herodias.

Herod and Herodias carry glaring similarities to Ahab and Jezebel. Herodias hated John the way Jezebel hated Elijah.

THE SPIRIT OF ELIJAH CONFRONTS ATROCITIES AND CULTURAL EVIL

Both John the Baptist and Jesus confronted the spirit of Jezebel. John went right at them, and Jesus responded to them. We must recognize that Jesus didn't come to take on the geopolitical structure of the day and rightsize it. He came *to seek and save the lost* (Luke 19:10). His mission was to first come as the Lamb of God. What should be seen, though, is that even as the Lamb of God, Jesus would not allow political threats to get in the way of His mission.

THE LAMB OF GOD DID NOT COME FOR POLITICAL WAR

There was a movement in those days run by a group of individuals known as "the zealots." These were strictly about taking back the government and fighting the powers that be. Historically, going to the time of the Maccabees and others who stood their ground against foreign adversaries, what some stood for when wanting to overthrow the government would have seemed like a good fit. And logically, it is something Jesus could have easily spoken up about.

However, it's important to clarify that Jesus had a different mission. His role was not to lead a political revolution but to fulfill prophecy. The political figures of the time were looking for a Messiah who would fulfill all the prophecies and take on the responsibility of governing, a role that Jesus was uniquely suited for.

THE LION YET TO APPEAR

While their understanding of the scriptures was correct, the time had not yet come for its fulfillment. The first advent had arrived, but we must be prepared for the second advent, when Jesus will not appear as the Lamb but as the Lion. All the prophecies about His governance will be fulfilled dramatically and unprecedentedly.

After establishing Jesus as the Lamb of God, who came to seek and save the lost, we turn to His response to the government. Unlike John the Baptist, who openly confronted Herod and Herodias, leading to his imprisonment, Jesus took a different approach.

Jesus, on the other hand, was known for statements such as "Render to Caesar what is Caesar's." Jesus told Peter that the sons of the kingdom were exempt from paying taxes, but He went on to provide a fish with a coin in its mouth to pay taxes for both Him and Peter.

When government overreach threatened His mission, Jesus spoke out derogatorily. A sliver of the Lion appeared and had a micro-flash moment.

A SLIVER APPEARANCE FROM THE LION

On that very day some Pharisees came, saying to Him, "Get out and depart from here, for Herod wants to kill You." ³² And He said to them, "Go, tell that fox, 'Behold, I cast out demons and perform cures today and tomorrow, and the third day I shall be perfected.'"

—Luke 13:31-32

The Pharisees cited authority to get Jesus off His assignment. Their strategy is straight out of religion's playbook or the religious structure that was married to the world. These types who have institutionalized a revelation have relegated what was once effective and life-giving to their gain. They only care about position, power, money, and control.

Jesus was not going to let the Pharisees and their Institutionalized Religion, citing government overreach, push Him around or off His mission.

JESUS CONFRONTING A FOX

The Pharisees tried to intimidate Jesus from their political standing. It was intimidation, telling Him *to stop* what He was doing because Big Brother wouldn't like it. These Pharisees were very religious and married to the political structure. Because of this, they would cite the Babylonian and hellish system of authority. They were pushing back on Jesus, saying, "Stop what You're doing. We're coming to You with the rule of law and the laws of the land. If You don't stop, Herod will get You."

Jesus' use of the words *that fox*: This was Herod Antipas, tetrarch of Galilee, whom Josephus described as a crafty and incestuous prince, with which the character given him by our Lord and the narratives of the evangelists coincide.

It is very interesting to note that this is the only person to whom Jesus spoke of in a derogatory manner. Herod had gone over the limit. Jesus had nothing to say to him except the message he sent, "You go tell that fox I'm going to do My work...."

The word for "fox" here is *vixen*, and means *a spirited or fierce woman, especially one seen as sexually attractive*. These words may have been pointed at the sly behavior of Herod, or they may have been a little deeper and directed at the one running things, the Jezebel, behind Herod's actions when he ordered the murder of John the Baptist. Jesus could have been sending a message to Herodias! Jesus could have been sending His response to the one in charge, the female leading the show and running things. It's possible Jesus was referring to Herod's perverse lifestyle. Whatever the point Jesus was making, He was telling them a message.

Jesus responded to the Pharisees, citing Herod, by saying, "No! I won't. Get out of My way. I have a job to do.⁴

BEWARE OF THE LEAVEN OF HEROD

Then He charged them, saying, "Take heed, beware of the leaven of the Pharisees and the leaven of Herod."

—Mark 8:15

Jesus commented on the doctrine of Herod or succumbing to the teaching or propaganda of the Herod administration.

> The Sadducees were sticklers for Herod, and his government, which the Pharisees had no good opinion of; or else distinct from one another; and so Christ cautions against the doctrines of the Pharisees, which regarded the traditions of the elders, and of the Sadducees, concerning the resurrection, and of the Herodians, who thought Herod to be the Messiah; and against the unreasonable request and demand of them all to have a sign from heaven, in proof of his own Messiahship.[5]

Here again we see Jesus talking about a political situation if it were causing His mission to be impacted.

JESUS DID MEET HEROD IN PERSON

> *Now when Herod saw Jesus, he was exceedingly glad; for he had desired for a long time to see Him, because he had heard many things about Him, and he hoped to see some miracle done by Him.* [9] *Then he questioned Him with many words, but He answered him nothing.*
>
> —Luke 23:8-9

Pilate sent Jesus to Herod, which made Herod happy. He had heard about Jesus and was curious. He wanted to see Jesus work a miracle. Herod asked Jesus many questions, but Jesus didn't say a word. He had no answers for Herod.

It is sad when a man's condition is so bad, such as Herod's, that the Lord has no words for him at all. Jesus refused to speak to him and had no word for him; that is how far he had gone. What a sad condition to be in.

The Matthew Henry commentary of Luke 13 says it well.

> His defiance of Herod's rage and the Pharisees' too; he fears neither the one nor the other: *Go you, and tell that fox so,* Luke 13:32. In calling him a *fox,* he gives him his true character; for he was subtle as a fox, noted for his craft, and treachery, and baseness, and preying (as they say of a fox) furthest from his own den. And, though it is a black and ugly character, yet it did not ill become Christ to give it to him, nor was it in him a violation of that law, *Thou shalt not speak evil of the ruler of thy people.*
>
> For Christ was a prophet, and prophets always had a liberty of speech in reproving princes and great men.
>
> Nay, Christ was more than a prophet, he was a king, he was King of kings, and the greatest of men were accountable to him, and therefore it became him to call this proud king by his own name; but it is not to be drawn into an example by us. "Go, and tell *that* fox, yea, and *this* fox too" (for so it is in the original, tē alōpeki tautē); "*that Pharisee,* whoever he is, that whispers this in my ear, let him know that *I do not fear him,* nor regard his menaces. For," 1. "I know that I must die, and must die shortly; I expect it, and count upon it, *the third day,*" that is, "very shortly; my hour is at hand."[6]

ELIJAH, BEFORE THE COMING OF THE GREAT AND TERRIBLE DAY OF THE LORD

Another day of judgment and tribulation is coming that will impact the entire world. The spirit of Elijah will once again come, but not on a person or another John the Baptist, but by the leading of the Holy Spirit to move His Church to stand at the appropriate times and speak at the right time.

Scripture does not teach us that Elijah will himself come again or that a person will once again embody that responsibility like John the Baptist. Instead, the called-out ones will be part of the end times, the last day's responsibility to fulfill the Great Commission and occupy until He returns.

Like Jesus, however, we should do so anywhere that agencies have a right to speak out to or push back against when they attempt to interrupt the Church's assignment. God has not called us to be timid and weak. He has called us to rescue the dying, give justice to the helpless, and preach the kingdom of God to every corner of the world. The day may come when we completely lose that ability due to a wicked dark kingdom dominating society.

If we have the liberty to speak today, we should do so to the glory of the Lord. It is our responsibility to choose our leaders wisely and push back against every satanic, Antichrist agenda to the glory of the Lord.

Let's recall how John the Baptist and Jesus stood in their time:

+ John the Baptist spoke up against Herod and Herodias.
+ Jesus called Herod a fox.
+ Jesus warned about Herod's deception.

We are called to be salt and light. The spirit of Elijah is one of preparation for the second coming of the Lord Jesus Christ!

CHAPTER SIX

SONS OF ISSACHAR
MANTLED TO WATCH
AND DISCERN

Of the sons of Issachar who had understanding of the times, to know what Israel ought to do, their chiefs were two hundred; and all their brethren were at their command.

—1 Chronicles 12:32

Understanding the time and season you are living in is, according to Jesus, the opposite of hypocrisy, and it is a requirement. Jesus mentioned this with direct clarity in Matthew 16:3 by saying, "…Hypocrites! You know how to discern the face of the sky, but you cannot discern the signs of the times." When referencing the sons of Issachar, most have an idea that they were the ones who knew the times or could indeed read the signs of the times. A point of interest is that the uniqueness of their ability to discern the signs of the times had two additional and crucial aspects to their operation.

WHO WERE THESE SONS OF ISSACHAR?

Issachar in Hebrew is *yiśśāskār.* He was Jacob's fifth son by Leah (Genesis 30:17-18; Genesis 35:23) and the seventh son of Obed-edom. He was a doorkeeper to the temple, and his name carries the meanings "man of hire" and "he will bring a reward." As a side note, Issachar is often paired with Zebulun (Genesis 49:13-14, Deuteronomy 33:18-19) and his wealth with maritime riches.

Issachar had four sons: Tola, Puah, Jashub, and Shimron (1 Chronicles 7:1). Through these four sons, the tribe grew, as is indicated in 1 Chronicles 7:1-5.

> The sons of Issachar were Tola, Puah, Jashub, and Shimron—four in all. ² The sons of Tola were Uzzi, Rephaiah, Jeriel, Jahmai, Jibsam, and Shemuel, heads of their father's house. The sons of Tola were mighty men of valor in their generations; their number in the days of David was twenty-two thousand six hundred. ³ The son of Uzzi was Izrahiah, and the sons of Izrahiah were Michael, Obadiah, Joel, and Ishiah. All five of them were chief men. ⁴ And with them, by their generations, according to their fathers' houses, were thirty-six thousand troops ready for war; for they had many wives and sons. ⁵ Now their brethren among all the families of Issachar were mighty men of valor, listed by their genealogies, eighty-seven thousand in all.
>
> **—1 Chronicles 7:1-5**

ISSACHAR UNDERSTOOD PUBLIC AFFAIRS

During David's reign, the tribe of Issachar provided many soldiers and leading commanders to the kingdom. These sons of Issachar understood public affairs, the nation's temper and zeitgeist, and the tendencies of present events. They also adhered to Saul while he lived.

THE SONS OF ISSACHAR
WAITED FOR KING DAVID

Recognizing that David had yet to take possession of the kingdom, they could not join him. Much of this was due to Abner, who commanded the other tribes surrounding Issachar. As soon as Saul died, they could declare themselves on the scene in favor of David and align with him as their king.

These men of Issachar were noted for their understanding and actions by the time of David (1 Chronicles 12:32). It is interesting to note that Issachar was allotted a place in Ezekiel's vision of a new Temple and a New Jerusalem, which has future ramifications (Ezekiel 48:25-33).[1]

IT COULD BE SAID
ISSACHAR HELPED GET
DAVID TO THE THRONE

These sons of Issachar were those who navigated the signs of the times. They were not necessarily in conflict with whichever administration was in power. Instead, their knowledge and understanding prepared them for the proper king to come. They prepared and awaited David's reign in the instance of Saul and David. That is, they were capable and intelligent men who understood the signs of the times, were well-versed in political affairs, and knew what was proper to be done in all the exigencies or current pressing, even urgent issues of human life in their generation, and during the time of Saul and David. These perceived that it was both the duty and in the best political interest of Israel to advance David to the throne. You might say they, with all their abilities, helped get David elected![2]

NOTABLE FIGURES FROM THE TRIBE OF ISSACHAR

Deborah

And the princes of Issachar were with Deborah; as Issachar, so was Barak sent into the valley under his command; among the divisions of Reuben there were great resolves of heart.

—Judges 5:15

Tola (a minor Judge)

After Abimelech there arose to save Israel Tola the son of Puah, the son of Dodo, a man of Issachar; and he dwelt in Shamir in the mountains of Ephraim.

—Judges 10:1

King Baasha (although he did evil, he was still listed in the lineage of Issachar)

Then Baasha the son of Ahijah, of the house of Issachar, conspired against him. And Baasha killed him at Gibbethon, which belonged to the Philistines, while Nadab and all Israel laid siege to Gibbethon.

—1 Kings 15:27

ASTRONOMERS, ASTROLOGERS, AND STATESMEN

Similar to the wise men or Chaldeans that Daniel oversaw and who ultimately found their way to Jesus, the sons of Issachar also operated by discerning the heavens and much more.

According to the *Targum*, the collection of Aramaic interpretative translations of the Old Testament was made when Hebrew had ceased to be the standard medium of speech among the Jews.[3]

> According to the Targum, they were all astronomers and astrologers: "and the sons of Issachar, who had understanding to know the times, and were skilled in fixing the beginnings of years, the commencement of months, and the intercalation of months and years; skillful in the changes of the moon, and in fixing the lunar solemnities to their proper times; skillful also in the doctrine of the solar periods; astrologers in signs and stars, that they might show Israel what to do; and their teachers were two hundred chiefs of the Sanhedrin: and all their brethren excelled in the words of the law, and were endued with wisdom, and were obedient to their command." –T.

> It appears that in their wisdom, experience, and skill, their brethren had the fullest confidence; and nothing was done but by their direction and advice.[4]

TRAITS OF ISSACHAR— UNDERSTANDING THE TIMES

According to the *Targum*, this extraordinary tribe had a unique and specialized set of skills. They had an understanding of the times. In

1 Chronicles 12:32 where it says, "of the sons of Issachar who *had* understanding of the times, to *know*," the Hebrew word for "had" and "know" is *yāḏaʿ* H3045: A verb meaning *to know, to learn, to perceive, to discern, to experience, to confess, to consider, to know people relationally, to know how, to be skillful, to be made known, to make oneself known, to make to known.*[5]

All these insightful and prophetic traits gave them a unique and highly trained ability to read the terrain of the current and upcoming seasons and their general narrative.

The *Targum* offers insights into the set of skills and points of operation by which the sons of Issachar operated. Consider the importance of what these traits mean and how they might, in some form, help us understand our generation's times and what to do about them.

TWELVE ISSACHARIAN TRAITS AS THEY APPLY TO THEIR SEASON

- Able to *learn*
- Able to *perceive*
- Able to *discern*
- Able to *experience*
- Able to *confess*
- Able to *consider*
- Able to *know people relationally*
- Able to *know how*
- Able to be *skillful*
- Able to *be made known*
- Able to *make oneself known*
- Able to *make to know*

THE DOOR OF REVELATORY UNDERSTANDING

Empirically, through their eyes and experiences, they would learn from the world around them, observing patterns and trends through their developed and trained mechanisms of discernment. One of the Hebrew pictographs for this Hebrew word, again observing the Hebrew word *yāda'*, we see that it also represents *a door* and *an eye*, meaning *the door of the eye.*[6]

The eye is the window into the human's very being. Experience and discernment are often gained through visual observation. Knowledge is achieved through these experiences, and revelation is acquired for those who have ears to hear.

TWO ORIGINS OF THE NAME ISSACHAR

It is fascinating to discover that Issachar comes from two words. First, there is a familiar word: the Hebrew word *nâsâ'* or *nasa*, a verb meaning *to lift, to carry, or to take away*. This verb is used almost six hundred times in the Hebrew Bible and covers three distinct semantic ranges. The second word is *sakar*, meaning *wages* or *reward*.

NASA

1. The meaning in its first range is to lift, which occurs in both literal (Genesis 7:17; Genesis 29:1; Ezekiel 10:16) and figurative statements: to lift the hand in taking an oath; in combat (2 Samuel 18:28); as a sign (Isaiah 49:22); in retribution (Psalm 10:12). Other figurative statements include the lifting of the head (Genesis 40:13); the face (2 Samuel 2:22); the eyes (Genesis 13:10); the voice (1 Samuel 30:4).

2. The second semantic category is to bear or to carry and is used especially in reference to the bearing of guilt or punishment of sin (Genesis 4:13; Leviticus 5:1). This flows easily then into the concept of the representative or substitutionary bearing of one person's guilt by another (Leviticus 10:17; Leviticus 16:22). The final category is to take away. It can be used in the simple sense of taking something (Genesis 27:3); to take a wife or to get married (Ruth 1:4); to take away guilt or to forgive (Genesis 50:17); to take away or to destroy (Job 32:22).

SAKAR

1. Meaning wages or reward; *he will bring a reward*; *Jissaskar*, a son of Jacob: Issachar.

2. This word also carries the idea of a seed representing *continuance*. Additionally, it carries the picture of a thorn representing the idea of grabbing hold. Combined, these means *continue to grab hold.*

3. Other meanings that go along with the name Issachar are the representation of a tribal flag that is hung from a horizontal pole and lifted up high and seen from a distance. The same could be stated for a flag or sail or banner that hangs from a pole.[7]

JESUS' DEFINITION OF HYPOCRITES!

Then the Pharisees and Sadducees came, and testing Him asked that He would show them a sign from heaven. ² He answered and said to them, "When it is evening you say, 'It will be fair weather, for the sky is red'; ³ and in the morning, 'It will be foul weather today, for the sky is red and threatening.' Hypocrites! You know how to discern the face of the sky, but you cannot discern the signs of the times. [4] *A wicked and adulterous generation seeks after a sign, and no sign shall be given to it except the sign of the prophet Jonah." And He left them and departed.*

—Matthew 16:1-4

Jesus made this statement with stark clarity by saying, "…Hypocrites! You know how to discern the face of the sky, but you cannot discern the signs of the times…." Jesus said, "If you can predict what the weather will be like and yet cannot perceive the days you are living in—you are a hypocrite!"

Why did He call them hypocrites? Because those who only look at what is unfolding around them from a natural standpoint deny a significant part of who they are or how God created them!

We were created to examine the world around us from both viewpoints—the natural and the Spirit. We were meant to understand, perceive, and discern the signs of the times.

CARNAL AND NATURAL-MINDED PEOPLE WALK IN BLINDNESS!

I say then: Walk in the Spirit, and you shall not fulfill the lust of the flesh.

—Galatians 5:16

Walking in the Spirit means walking in God's Word. Jesus, after all, said His words were Spirit in John 6:63. What must be understood is the flesh. What does the Bible mean by flesh or carnality? The flesh is a way of thinking that opposes God's Word. The flesh is a mindset not led by the Word of God but by the five senses. Regarding the signs of the times, anyone who can see what the weather will produce but not what is happening on the eternal timetable or in their time is a hypocrite, only engaging the natural carnal part of their being.

A good example of this would be a person who looks at the natural by only watching the news and what are common, normal markers to navigate through life. Sadly, from their intellect and natural persuasions, most people live 100 percent of their time on earth. They believe nothing unless it is scientifically verified and proven from every angle. Even then, they look through the meat glasses of carnality.

THE RICH MAN AND LAZARUS

There was a certain rich man who was clothed in purple and fine linen and fared sumptuously every day. [20] *But there was a certain beggar named Lazarus, full of sores, who was laid at his gate,* [21] *desiring to be fed with the crumbs which fell from the rich man's table. Moreover the dogs came and licked his sores.* [22] *So it was that the beggar died, and was carried by the angels to Abraham's bosom. The rich man also died and was buried.* [23] *And being in torments in Hades, he lifted up his eyes and saw Abraham afar off, and Lazarus in his bosom.* [24] *Then he cried and said, "Father Abraham, have mercy on me, and send Lazarus that he may dip the tip of his finger in water and cool my tongue; for I am tormented in this flame."* [25] *But Abraham said, "Son, remember that in your lifetime you received your good things, and likewise Lazarus evil things; but now he is comforted and you are tormented.* [26] *And besides all this, between*

*us and you there is a great gulf fixed, so that those who
want to pass from here to you cannot, nor can those from
there pass to us." ²⁷ Then he said, 'I beg you therefore,
father, that you would send him to my father's house, ²⁸
for I have five brothers, that he may testify to them, lest
they also come to this place of torment." ²⁹ Abraham said
to him, "They have Moses and the prophets; let them
hear them." ³⁰ And he said, "No, father Abraham; but
if one goes to them from the dead, they will repent." ³¹
But he said to him, "If they do not hear Moses and the
prophets, neither will they be persuaded though one rise
from the dead."*

—**Luke 16:19-31**

Consider the rich man and Lazarus. Interestingly, part of this story parallels what Jesus was conveying about those who see the world only through the natural lens.

Amazingly, Jesus, by telling the story of Lazarus and the rich man, comes to the part where the rich man, who was in hell, begs Father Abraham to send an angel or someone back from the dead to tell the rich man's living relatives about the horrors of hell. This story shows what happens to departed souls who have not called on the Name of the Lord. It also conveys a powerful truth even through the dazzling of the five senses, with shocking empirical evidence of the supernatural, such as someone coming back from the dead to testify of what awaits after death. Even such an encounter would not make the recipients believe if they did not already believe the scriptures. Again, as Abraham stated in Luke 16:31, "If they do not hear Moses and the prophets, neither will they be persuaded though one rise from the dead."

Miracles without the Word of God following do not provide sustaining power. The rich man asked for the equivalent of his idea of the ultimate magic act—shock them, dazzle them, and then they will believe. Ultimately, this was his thought process and belief system.

ABRAHAM'S RESPONSE

And he said, "No, father Abraham; but if one goes to them from the dead, they will repent." [31] *But he said to him, "If they do not hear Moses and the prophets, neither will they be persuaded though one rise from the dead."*

—Luke 16:30-31

The rich man pleaded and negotiated with Abraham, saying *if you will send Lazarus or send someone back from the dead*—then *people would believe!* The rich man wrongly said *God has not done a good enough job!* The rich man might as well have said, "If you would do it the way I am saying to do it, then they would listen!"

The rich man displayed his hardness of heart, saying that if you give them irrefutable scientific evidence, they will believe. Where the words of Jesus clearly state, "Blessed are those who believe without seeing" (see John 20:29).

God desires to be believed without Him painting things in crayon for the five senses to grasp in every imaginable way. However, if you read and believe the Bible, all things available to know by the Spirit will become illuminated.

MAN LOOKS TO THE NATURAL, BUT GOD OPERATES BY FAITH

My point in comparing the two scenarios is that man always looks to the natural or carnal side for evidence and truth. In contrast, God is a Spirit, and those who worship Him must do so in Spirit and truth! (See John 4:24.) Another way of looking at this would be to say that God is more interested in you believing Him before He has to prove Himself to you.

Remember Thomas, who said, "Unless I see in His hands the print of the nails, and put my finger into the print of the nails, and put my hand into His side, I will not believe" (John 20:25).

In a gracious accommodation, Jesus allowed Thomas to do those very things (see John 20:27). I believe Jesus allowed this because He already had a relationship with Thomas. What is vital, however, is not to be led by the carnal point of view but rather by a point of view filled with and operated by the Spirit of God.

THERE CAN BE ONLY ONE MASTER!

For those who live according to the flesh set their minds on the things of the flesh, but those who live according to the Spirit, the things of the Spirit. [6] For to be carnally minded is death, but to be spiritually minded is life and peace. [7] Because the carnal mind is enmity against God; for it is not subject to the law of God, nor indeed can be. [8] So then, those who are in the flesh cannot please God. [9] But you are not in the flesh but in the Spirit, if indeed the Spirit of God dwells in you. Now if anyone does not have the Spirit of Christ, he is not His.

—Romans 8:5-9

The carnal mind or way of thinking that goes against the Word of God cannot please God. Romans 8:6 blatantly says, "To be carnally minded is death, but to be spiritually minded is life and peace."

What a statement! Verse 7 says, "Because the carnal mind is enmity against God, for it is not subject to the law of God, nor indeed can be." Carnal-mindedness is to be in direct opposition to God and how His laws operate! That is why Paul further states that those in the flesh cannot please God.

In Matthew 16, Jesus confronted the same issue by calling them hypocrites! He was saying, "Stop being carnal and see with the eyes of the Spirit!"

HOW TO DEVELOP DISCERNMENT

Hypocrite! First remove the plank from your own eye, and then you will see clearly to remove the speck from your brother's eye.

—**Matthew 7:5**

When referencing the sons of Issachar, most have an idea that they were the ones who knew the times or could indeed read the signs of the times. A point of interest is that the uniqueness of their ability to discern the signs of the times has two scriptural and crucial aspects to their operation.

We must avoid hypocrisy to better discern the signs of the times. Jesus didn't call those who could not discern the signs of the times blind, sinners, or some other name; He called them hypocrites.

The word here for "hypocrite" means *one who acts pretentiously, a counterfeit, a man who assumes and speaks or acts under a feigned character.*[8]

HYPOCRITES OR ACTORS ON A STAGE

My dear friend and Greek expert Rick Renner has defined Jesus' use of the word "hypocrite" to refer to actors on a stage. The word "hypocrite" means *one who wears a mask or walks in a pretense*. It was used to denote actors on the stage who acted the part and did anything for the applause of the crowd but were different behind the mask they wore.

The term "hypocrite" was a reference Jesus would have gained while working in Sepphoris alongside his earthly father, Joseph.

Sepphoris had a very modern and active culture. It was a city on a hill.

When Jesus was still a child, there was an uprising against Archelaus, Herod's son, who had to summon the Roman army. The Romans destroyed Sepphoris and crucified two thousand Jews in the process. It is this uprising that Gamaliel refers to in Acts 5:37.[9]

Here is an excerpt about Sepphoris from my book *Breaking Hell's Economy*:

> After the destruction of Sepphoris, it was rebuilt and needed builders like Joseph to reconstruct the ruined city. Joseph was raising Jesus in Nazareth, which was about an hour's walk from Sepphoris, so Joseph, being a builder, would take Jesus with him to work there. It was during these trips that Jesus learned about business and money. He was exposed to the world of theater in this once-again booming town where entertainment was vibrant, with people performing on stages along the roadsides.
>
> Actors on a stage were referred to as "hypocrites" while performing. This was terminology Jesus used while

speaking to the Pharisees. Applying this cultural understanding, Jesus said, "You hypocrites!" or "You actors on a stage!" He also crafted lines such as "A city on a hill that cannot be hidden" during His teachings. This came from seeing Sepphoris, the city on the hill with its lights and vibrancy while living in Nazareth. Jesus had all these examples in mind because he helped His earthly father with his business.

Jesus saw a lot of things at Sepphoris. Imagine Jesus as a young boy, potentially walking past those rebels who were crucified in town by the Romans. He likely saw the bodies of those rebels nailed on crosses, knowing deep within Himself that something similar awaited Him. History doesn't tell us much about the young life of Jesus; neither does the Bible. However, by combining historical narratives with the Bible, you can discover otherwise elusive information about the childhood of Jesus.[10]

HIGH-LEVEL DISCERNMENT MEANS REMOVE THE PLANK!

Hypocrite! First remove the plank from your own eye, and then you will see clearly to remove the speck from your brother's eye.

—**Matthew 7:5**

Walking at the highest level of discernment means removing the plank from your eye. Much of this involves the idea that you are something more than you are. Or you are holding yourself in a high place when you ought not to do so. That is what Paul called deceiving oneself.

> *For if anyone thinks himself to be something, when he is nothing, he deceives himself.*
>
> **—Galatians 6:3**

Extracting hypocrisy and stepping into clarity means removing the plank of self-centeredness and self-exaltation, pretending to be something you are not, and taking it out of your life. Selflessness and loving your brethren are the most significant foundations of clarity.

One final thought on hypocrisy being the opposite of discerning the signs of the times is noticing that hypocrisy involves a plank in the eye. Jesus could have used a variety of metaphors when speaking about hypocrisy. Still, He chose to reference a plank in the eye—the area of sight being blocked—no vision, no clarity, and only using one eye. When only one eye is in use due to a plank being in the other, it cuts a person's range of view down by at least 50 percent.

It could be that Jesus was saying hypocrisy will cause you to see with one eye but not the other, or you can see in the natural but not the spirit. Remove the plank of hypocrisy, begin discerning the times, and open the part of you that should see what is happening in your generation by the spiritual sight God has given every person who believes in Jesus and will exercise their spiritual senses (see Hebrews 5:14).

THREE MAIN THINGS THE SONS OF ISSACHAR DID

Of the sons of Issachar who had understanding of the times, to know what Israel ought to do, their chiefs were two hundred; and all their brethren were at their command.

—1 Chronicles 12:32

The sons of Issachar *understood the times, knew what Israel should do,* and *had the proper alignment and structure to act.* Interpreting the times involves more than simply recognizing what is happening worldwide. Proper alignment and a plan of action are also required. They had their chiefs and brethren at their command—these were their people. They knew who their tribe was, which allowed them to carry out what needed to be done.

I often say, "God doesn't call you to live wherever you choose. You must make sure you are where God has called you. If you do not know, seeking Him over His will for your life is vital."

God can supernaturally align you to who, what, where, when, and how you are to walk out the times and seasons in which you live. Start seeking Him today, re-sensitize your heart to His Word and what the Holy Spirit is leading you to do. It's only forever![11]

CHAPTER SEVEN

AGENTS OF TIME
EXTENSION, SUSPENSION, AND INTERVENTION

He saw that there was no man, and wondered that there was no intercessor; therefore His own arm brought salvation for Him; and His own righteousness, it sustained Him.

—Isaiah 59:16

Every generation has significant defining moments marshaled by good or evil powers. Knowing this, it becomes crucial to recognize that both God and the devil are territorial. They advance their agendas through the cooperation of natural human beings. We know there is no comparison or competition between God and the devil. Yet there are laws by which all spiritual beings must operate.

We call natural human beings free moral agents who, through their belief systems and actions, align with and even allow the corresponding spiritual forces to work through them. These agents can impact the culture by working through them.

Jesus answered, "Most assuredly, I say to you, unless one is born of water and the Spirit, he cannot enter the

THE SPIRIT OF ELIJAH

kingdom of God. ⁶ That which is born of the flesh is flesh,
and that which is born of the Spirit is spirit."

—John 3:5-6

In John 3:5-6, Jesus explained that a person is born of water and then of Spirit. What needs to be understood by every believer specifically is that to be born again or saved, one must first be born of water. What does that mean? In simple terms, it means to be born of a woman. You must be born of flesh and blood passing through the water.

When a woman's water breaks, the birth of a baby is not far behind. This is where every person comes from. To put it in simpler terms, every person on earth has something spirits do not have—*physical bodies.*

PHYSICAL BODIED REPRESENTATIVES

Love has been perfected among us in this: that we may
have boldness in the day of judgment; because as He is, so
are we in this world.

—1 John 4:17

God can do what He desires on earth through His people who live in physical bodies. These are free moral agents who can accomplish in the natural what spirits cannot do. As spirits are not authorized to operate on the earth without physical authority, only possessors of physical bodies can accomplish things in the natural world. God desires to bring forth defining moments for a culture for its good and benefit. To achieve this, God has chosen to work through human beings, which can be a very limiting scope. This is why preaching the gospel of the kingdom is crucial to see God's will done on earth as it is in heaven.

However, the same is true of darkness. Evil also has a plan, which is ushered in through the agents with physical bodies operating on wickedness' behalf. These arrive to wreak havoc, to steal, kill, and destroy a culture.

HUMANS ARE THE GATEKEEPERS TO THE NATURAL WORLD

Significant defining events and moments present themselves for territorial gain, and these moments are often contended over. Those with physical bodies or free moral agents collide and fight the battles. This means that human beings can decide who they will serve. In modern society, human beings are the ones who cause events that may vary in form, such as global black swan scenarios (these are rare, unexpected adverse events that affect the world and can range from financial crashes, natural disasters, or terrorist attacks), more minor localized issues, riots, political takeovers, genocide, or any other evil thing. Of course, those on the Lord's side are agents for all things good and constructive, ultimately advancing the gospel of the kingdom.

Such battles are fought for territory, both in cities and nations, and for the mindset or what could be labeled the zeitgeist of society. Additionally, battles are fought over defining moments in history, such as the battles for global control in World War II or the events leading up to the fall of the Berlin Wall. Consider the defining moments leading up to the abolishment of slavery. Many moments from ancient world history until now have defining moments won or lost based on the actions of free moral agents. The bottom line is that we must influence as many as we can to cooperate with the will of God.

DEFINING MOMENTS IN TIME

Mount Carmel was a defining moment in time. It was a territorial battle that would determine who the real God of the nation was. Baal and the Living God of the universe would collide, and the representatives of each power structure were on the scene. Light sought to triumph over the dark. However, the light required a reformer, an agent of the time.

Agents of God, reformers, step into these circumstances or collisions to determine which force will have its will accomplished. These agents rise and carry a knowing, like the sons of Issachar, to alter the scenario or disrupt the plans of evil to see the purpose of the Lord accomplished.

Consider the story of Abraham when the Lord was visiting him. God's man of that time was Abraham, an intercessor for what the Lord would do on the earth. As we progress into this chapter, I ask that you, dear reader, consider what God has called you to do. You are a significant part of His plan for humanity and even carry the potential to alter certain things as it pertains to "when" the Lord is doing something in the land or your generation. Is it possible that believers—free moral agents of the Most High Living God might be able to alter some things in the timing of when they might happen? Let's find out together.

> Then the men rose from there and looked toward Sodom, and Abraham went with them to send them on the way. [17] And the LORD said, "Shall I hide from Abraham what I am doing, [18] since Abraham shall surely become a great and mighty nation, and all the nations of the earth shall be blessed in him? [19] For I have known him, in order that he may command his children and his household after him, that they keep the way of the LORD, to do righteousness

and justice, that the LORD may bring to Abraham what He has spoken to him." [20] And the LORD said, "Because the outcry against Sodom and Gomorrah is great, and because their sin is very grave, [21] I will go down now and see whether they have done altogether according to the outcry against it that has come to Me; and if not, I will know."

—**Genesis 18:16-21**

ABRAHAM ATTEMPTED TO EXTEND SODOM AND GOMORRAH'S SEASON— SUSPENDING JUDGMENT

Then he said, "Let not the Lord be angry, and I will speak but once more: Suppose ten should be found there?" And He said, "I will not destroy it for the sake of ten."

—**Genesis 18:32**

Abraham went on to entreat the Lord to save the city, starting with the number 50 as a reason for Sodom and Gomorrah not to be destroyed. Abraham was bold enough to ask God for anything from 50 to 10.

If Abraham had been bolder, God might have spared the city even for one—we may never know this side of eternity. However, we know it is God's nature to rescue and show mercy, and He looks for those who will appeal to Him for what He will do.

Especially in the New Testament era, we must remember "the Great Commission." God has not called us to the great "mission" but "the Great Co-Mission." Together with Him, we cooperate to fulfill His desire on earth.

BIBLE PROPHECY CANNOT BE STOPPED, BUT CAN TIME BE ADJUSTED?

Prophecy cannot be stopped, and what the Bible says cannot be altered. Having said this, I would like to present what scripture shows us regarding seasons, intervention, and the suspension of what is set in motion, even offering an interesting question about God and time.

Through scripture, I desire to suggest that it may be possible for agents of God, reformers, or those doing His will on earth to alter the timing or the original plan for a particular event in certain circumstances.

Again, I want to reiterate that scripture and the prophecies laid out for us in scripture cannot be stopped. There is room for consideration that God looks for His people to get involved in what He is doing and loves it when we hold up His Word to Him and commune with Him about the events around us.

ABRAHAM MOVED THE NEEDLE IN GOD'S PLAN TO ANNIHILATE SODOM AND GOMORRAH

He saw that there was no man, and wondered that there was no intercessor; therefore His own arm brought salvation for Him; and His own righteousness, it sustained Him.

—Isaiah 59:16

Abraham negotiated with God for ten righteous; it wasn't enough to rescue the city as ten righteous were not found. However, we must consider that Abraham moved the needle from over 50 to 10! Abraham was *interceding* or *intervening* on behalf of his nephew Lot. There is a secret to altering the playing field and a long-planned, even overdue event of correction. Here is the secret—God wants to be conversed with. He is willing for all people to be saved and has always looked for a mediator in one fashion or another until He got the ultimate perfect mediator, Jesus.

GOD WANTS AN INTERCESSOR!

Run to and fro through the streets of Jerusalem; see now and know; and seek in her open places if you can find a man, if there is anyone who executes judgment, who seeks the truth, and I will pardon her.

—Jeremiah 5:1

"Now therefore, let Me alone, that My wrath may burn hot against them, and I may consume them. And I will make of you a great nation." [11] Then Moses pleaded with the LORD his God, and said: "LORD, why does Your wrath burn hot against Your people whom You have brought out of the land of Egypt with great power and with a mighty hand? [12] Why should the Egyptians speak, and say, 'He brought them out to harm them, to kill them in the mountains, and to consume them from the face of the earth'? Turn from Your fierce wrath, and relent from this harm to Your people. [13] Remember Abraham, Isaac, and Israel, Your servants, to whom You swore by Your own self, and said to them, 'I will multiply your descendants as the stars of heaven; and all this land that I have spoken of I give to your descendants, and they shall inherit

it forever.'" [14] So the LORD relented from the harm which He said He would do to His people.

—**Exodus 32:10-14**

Therefore He said that He would destroy them, had not Moses His chosen one stood before Him in the breach, to turn away His wrath, lest He destroy them.

—**Psalm 106:23**

Then the LORD said to me, "Even if Moses and Samuel stood before Me, My mind would not be favorable toward this people. Cast them out of My sight and let them go forth."

—**Jeremiah 15:1**

GOD COULD NOT FIND AN INTERCESSOR, SO, HE COUNTED ON HIMSELF

Conversing with God about any event is a sign to Him that He has an intercessor. Jesus the Lord is our ultimate intercessor and mediator. In the Old Testament era, we see examples of frustration when there was no intercessor. Thankfully, Jesus came and became the ultimate intercessor, the Great High Priest, making intercession for all of us day and night. It might be said that no person was found to be an effective intercessor for saving humankind, so God the Father and Christ Jesus the Son looked to themselves to answer humanity's plight.

SEASONS, INTERVENTION, AND SUSPENSIONS

As intercessors or those about the Father's business in their generation, there are certain graces and accesses to the power of God. Obedience creates boldness, and so does revelation. Those who walk in the revelation of who God is and what God can do are clear and strong. A weaponization of that revelation activates when there is a realization that God wants to work through you!

Under God's obedience, reformers can use their free moral agency to do the impossible. Something outstanding can transpire when there is a radical connection to God the Father and His will being done on earth as in heaven. Much like Abraham, who asked God not to go through with His judgment against Sodom and Gomorrah, although judgment was still poured out on that place, Abraham did move the needle as to how many God would pass the cities for—10. God would have bypassed scorching those places if ten righteous individuals were found. I suspect our great God might have gone down to one if Abraham had the boldness to ask. Full-scale apocalyptic fire and brimstone were still dropped on those wicked twin cities, but the point is Abraham moved the scale with the number of righteous people it would require for the Lord to show mercy.

GOD DESIRES A MEDIATOR

Again, God wants to have a mediator, someone who cares, one who stands as a voice in the land that will carry His heart for things, and who, as a free moral agent, a human being, will allow God to take action by permission from the very laws He created. Intercessors or those who know the rules of engagement as it works with the realm of the spirit and the natural can allow the Spirit of the Lord to have access to scenarios that would otherwise not be possible without violating His

Word. After all, God gave dominion over this world to man. Man, in turn, gave it over to the devil.

> And so it is written, "*The first man Adam became a living being.*" The last Adam became a life-giving spirit. [46] However, the spiritual is not first, but the natural, and afterward the spiritual. [47] The first man was of the earth, made of dust; the second Man is the Lord from heaven.
>
> —1 Corinthians 15:45-47

First Corinthians 15:45-47 illuminates what I am saying regarding humanity's authority. Adam was a man in God's image placed here on earth. He fell and lost his authority to the devil. As a result, the only way God could access the realm of this natural world was to come as a man. This is where Jesus, the Son of the Most High Living God, enters. Jesus came as a man to take what the devil stole from the first man. A lot could be said about this passage in 1 Corinthians 15:46, which states, "The spiritual is not first, but the natural, and afterward the spiritual...."

One takeaway is that the spiritual doesn't have first authority; instead, the natural does as it relates to man's domain. In the natural domain of man, God gave Adam authority over the Garden and was told to be fruitful and multiply. When Adam stepped into what many call "original sin" by listening to the talking serpent, he fell under the dominion of the devil. Why? Because he listened to the devil's voice over God's command to not eat of the tree. Adam not only listened, but he acted along with his wife, Eve. God's word was put to the side, and the devil was adhered to.

Jesus came as the last Adam, as a man to legally take back what the devil took from the first Adam.

Throughout history, events have been altered by the presence and actions of one of God's people, such as Abraham, and how he reduced the number of righteous to 10.

INTERRUPTIONS OF TIME

Time, space, and what is perceived as usual may all be adjustable by allowing the Architect and Builder of everything access to the moment. Alterations can be made to whatever circumstance God is invited into. Where this starts and stops is a place of speculation, and the line might be blurry at best, so I will simply reference what the Bible says about these kinds of scenarios.

The normal operation of this world's realities can experience interruptions to introduce God's will. This is largely dependent on a free moral agent who will enforce God's will for a situation and, by faith, alter things until the natural bow to the Spirit and unimaginable things become possible.

JOSHUA SUSPENDED TIME

Then Joshua spoke to the LORD in the day when the LORD delivered up the Amorites before the children of Israel, and he said in the sight of Israel: "Sun, stand still over Gibeon; and Moon, in the Valley of Aijalon." [13] *So the sun stood still, and the moon stopped, till the people had revenge upon their enemies. Is this not written in the Book of Jasher? So the sun stood still in the midst of heaven, and did not hasten to go down for about a whole day.* [14] *And there has been no day like that, before it or*

after it, that the LORD heeded the voice of a man; for the
LORD fought for Israel.

—Joshua 10:12-14

Joshua battled several enemy kings, defeating them in some interesting ways. A meteor shower had slaughtered more enemies than
Israel's soldiers did! The more significant part and one of the most
unique instances in scripture came next, and this was due to the need
to finish the job of killing off the remnants of these enemies so they
would not continue. In this instance, God lengthened the day—at
Joshua's command!

In Joshua 10:12, we see that Joshua commanded the sun and the
moon to "stand still."

Imagine this! What a moment! Joshua commanded the sun and the
moon in the Valley of Ajalon to stand at attention, extending the day
from what we can perceive as one whole day. This action was necessary
for Joshua and his army to have the time to destroy their enemies.

Thinking this instance through creates several questions. Did the
earth stop turning? Was its rotation at a halt? If so, this could lead to
radical tides, limitless flooding, and a whole host of issues all around
the planet.

I appreciate Chuck Missler's observations regarding questions and
an alternative approach to answering them: "What would happen if
the earth stopped rotating? What types of issues would come with
such a moment?"

> ...there is another possibility: a change in the precession
> of the earth would also lengthen an apparent day. Most
> ancient calendars were based on 360-day years. Yet all
> ancient calendars seem to change about 701 B.C. Some-
> thing caused the calendars to be revised. The Romans

added five and one-fourth days, in effect, but Hezekiah added a whole month to the Jewish calendar: seven times in a nineteen-year period, a rather weird formula. The rabbis speculate as to why he did it that way, but they don't explain why he had to change it in the first place.[1]

According to Chuck Missler, ancient calendars align with Joshua's account of stopping time for measuring a day.

When something needed to happen for the good of Joshua's generation, the amount of daylight was standing in the way of their success. God's man, His free moral agent committed to Him, spoke to the sun, commanding it to stop moving so that Joshua might finish his assignment.

Joshua 10:14 tells us another astonishing part: "...the LORD heeded the voice of a man; for the LORD fought for Israel." Joshua changed the time and season, even if for only a day! It made history and messed up calendars worldwide, so they had to adjust to that strange occurrence. Powerful moments occur when a generational reformer stands against any natural thing holding back the will of God, just like David and Goliath.

ISAIAH POTENTIALLY ALTERED TIME

"Behold, I will bring the shadow on the sundial, which has gone down with the sun on the sundial of Ahaz, ten degrees backward." So the sun returned ten degrees on the dial by which it had gone down.

—**Isaiah 38:8**

Then Isaiah said, "This is the sign to you from the LORD, that the LORD will do the thing which He has spoken: shall the shadow go forward ten degrees or go backward ten degrees?" [10] *And Hezekiah answered, "It is an easy thing for the shadow to go down ten degrees; no, but let the shadow go backward ten degrees."* [11] *So Isaiah the prophet cried out to the LORD, and He brought the shadow ten degrees backward, by which it had gone down on the sundial of Ahaz.*

—2 Kings 20:9-11

Bringing the shadow on the sundial backward symbolized a prophetic alteration of nature, divine healing, and the extension of Hezekiah's life.

Here, we find another unique instance in scripture of altering the sun, potentially time, or it might have been an eclipse. Whatever it was, we can ascertain that Isaiah cried out to the Lord, and the shadow moved in an unnatural direction—backward. Second Kings 20:11 says, "He [God] brought the shadow ten degrees backward...." Regardless of the event, we can see from the scripture that the Lord caused it.

A SUNDIAL

Interestingly, the sundial is the first means of marking time referenced in the Bible. A sundial was a Babylonian invention made of lines on a dial plate. Its purpose was to show the sun's progress and time of day. It was an early clock.

Some surmise that only the shadow itself was brought back by the power of God. That there was no altering of the sun or anything else. Everything in the sky and heavens keeps its course as usual, but in the following clause, the sun is expressly said to "return ten degrees."

Although all things are possible with the God who made the universe, it is still not easy to conceive how the *shadow of the sun* should go back—unless the sun itself did.

If it were only the shadow of the sun on Ahaz's dial, it would not have fallen under the notice and attention of other nations, nor would it have been the subject of their inquiry, as it was of the Babylonians in 2 Chronicles 32:31, "However, regarding the ambassadors of the princes of Babylon, whom they sent to him to inquire about the wonder that was done in the land, God withdrew from him, in order to test him, that He might know all that was in his heart."[2]

THE CRIES OF ISAIAH MAY HAVE CAUSED A SOLAR ECLIPSE

Ancient historian Josephus wrote about these degrees on the sundial, which were steps ascending to the palace of Ahaz; the time of day was indicated by the number of steps reached by the shadow. This sundial was of such size and visibility and positioned at the right line of sight that Hezekiah may have personally witnessed this miracle from his chamber.

Some believe the shadow moving backward may have been affected by refraction. A cloud denser than the air would interpose between the gnomon or metal right-angled fin, on which the sun would shine and cast a shadow directly onto the dial. Refraction from a cloud could cause the phenomenon. This does not detract from the miracle, for God gave him the choice of whether the shadow should go forward or back and regulated the time and place.

689 BC, THE YEAR OF A SOLAR ECLIPSE

Bosanquet makes the fourteenth year of Hezekiah 689 BC. Consequently, it is the known year of a solar eclipse. A solar eclipse could have happened when Isaiah cried out to the Lord, which is a natural explanation for the recession of the shadow.

God will answer His people one way or another using nature or materialize an unexplainable miracle to meet His agents about His business.[3]

MOSES AND TIME TRAVEL "ACHOR" NARRATIVE

And he said, "Please, show me Your glory." [19] Then He said, "I will make all My goodness pass before you, and I will proclaim the name of the LORD before you. I will be gracious to whom I will be gracious, and I will have compassion on whom I will have compassion." [20] But He said, "You cannot see My face; for no man shall see Me, and live." [21] And the LORD said, "Here is a place by Me, and you shall stand on the rock. [22] So it shall be, while My glory passes by, that I will put you in the cleft of the rock, and will cover you with My hand while I pass by. [23] Then I will take away My hand, and you shall see My back; but My face shall not be seen."

—Exodus 33:18-23

One of the ultimate biblical time-bending narratives may be found when Moses famously asked the Lord to show him His Glory! In Exodus 33:23, the word "back" is very interesting. Here is why Moses is known for writing the Bible's first five books. The only issue is that many scholars say that is an impossibility.

God's use of the word "back" is the Hebrew word *'âchôr*. It means *behind, backward; also (as facing north) the West: after (-ward), back (part, -side, -ward), hereafter, (be-) hind (-er part), time to come, without. It indicates direction, such as before, behind, or backward. It also can temporally refer to the future.*

When God said, "You shall see My back." It would have been impossible for anyone to see the beginning of creation unless God showed it to them. Therefore, God may very well have been showing Moses His great works from the beginning, such as the creation of the world and the fall of man. When Moses saw the glory of the Lord and the back (*'âchôr*) of God, the first thing he may have seen was darkness, a formless void, and darkness upon the face of the deep.

Moses then would have witnessed the Spirit of God moving upon the face of the deep, and while looking into the darkness, Moses heard the powerful words of God, *"Let there be light!"*

> And the earth was without form, and void; and darkness was upon the face of the deep. And the Spirit of God moved upon the face of the waters. ³ Then God said, Let there be light: and there was light.
>
> **—Genesis 1:2-3 KJV**

Moses would later write the words, *"In the beginning..."*

GOD IS MULTIDIMENSIONAL

How would Moses write Genesis 1, for example? Have you ever considered that? It asks how he captured the events of those early times in such detail. After all, he wasn't there. Or was he? Some scholars assume that Moses learned of the beginning through a form of oral tradition passed down by storytelling about the creation narrative and all events in prehistory. By this method, Moses recorded it. The detail Moses brings us in the narrative sounds like an eyewitness account.

In the light of Exodus 33, and when we consider that God is multidimensional as He alone is the Master of all creation, including time itself, this narrative takes on a very interesting possibility.

There is more to be conveyed in this story because the Hebrew word used for "back" (*âchôr*) has more meaning than simply looking into the past. As if looking to the past, answering the prehistory sections of the Torah isn't impressive enough. Still, an additional insight into the word (*âchôr*) opens another possibility—it can also temporally refer to the future. That's right, the future! How does this apply to Moses?

Is it possible that God, in the exact moment of showing Moses His back, both locationally and in former works of old, also pivoted, took Moses away from viewing the events of prehistory and began turning Moses in another direction through both location, space, and time to a future time? Perhaps to a mountain which would have been in a future time from the hour Moses was gazing at the glory of the Lord. According to what this word (*âchôr*) means, Moses was likely taken in the spirit to the north, where he was seeing and experiencing the Glory of the Lord.

When shown the Glory of God, is it possible that Moses saw both the beginning and was transported through time and space to the Mount of Transfiguration?

And, behold, there talked with him two men, which were Moses and Elias.

—Luke 9:30 KJV

And there appeared unto them Elias with Moses: and they were talking with Jesus.

—Mark 9:4 KJV

And, behold, there appeared unto them Moses and Elias talking with him.

—Matthew 17:3 KJV

That is an interesting thought, for sure! It is certainly open for speculation, but could it be that God may have introduced Moses to Jesus in person?

It is not a proven fact, but it is interesting to consider. We do know that Moses was there on the Mount of Transfiguration. You be the judge and discern it for yourself. God is multidimensional, and relating to Him as a Spirit is powerful. Through the prophetic, God can show His people things that have happened and have yet to occur.

Remember, God rules outside of time. He sees the end from the beginning, and knowing Him more through His Holy Spirit can make His secrets available to you—even if they are outside of time and space.[4]

JESUS SHARED AN INSIGHT TO PRAYER AND THE TIMELINES OF PROPHECY

Matthew 24 Sabbath and Wintertime prayer.

"Therefore when you see the 'abomination of desolation,' spoken of by Daniel the prophet, standing in the holy place" (whoever reads, let him understand), [16] *"then let those who are in Judea flee to the mountains.* [17] *Let him*

who is on the housetop not go down to take anything out of his house. [18] *And let him who is in the field not go back to get his clothes.* [19] *But woe to those who are pregnant and to those who are nursing babies in those days!* [20] *And pray that your flight may not be in winter or on the Sabbath."*

—**Matthew 24:15-20**

Jesus said, "Pray that your flight may not be in winter or on the Sabbath." Why would Jesus say to pray if He told them the prophetic things were ultimately fate? We know that prophecy from Jesus will always come to pass, no matter what. However, this small understanding has potentially massive implications. If we pray, Jesus suggests that we might be able to alter the timing of something. This is something to think about for any reformer, sons of Issachar, or those acting as free moral agents to their generation. To walk in the spirit of Elijah, we must be prepared to make an impact and change what everyone around us says is impossible to change!

IS THE TIMETABLE OF THE LORD'S RETURN MOVABLE?

But, beloved, do not forget this one thing, that with the Lord one day is as a thousand years, and a thousand years as one day. [9] *The Lord is not slack concerning His promise, as some count slackness, but is longsuffering toward us, not willing that any should perish but that all should come to repentance.* [10] *But the day of the Lord will come as a thief in the night, in which the heavens will pass away with a great noise, and the elements will melt with fervent heat; both the earth and the works that are in it will be burned up.* [11] *Therefore, since all these things will be dissolved, what manner of persons ought you to be in holy conduct and godliness, [12] looking for and hastening the coming of the day of God, because of which the heavens will be dissolved, being on fire, and the elements will melt with fervent heat?*

—**2 Peter 3:8-12**

Peter says we can hasten the coming of the Lord. How? Through our holy conduct and godliness. According to our placement or conduct with godliness, we might have a corporate part in expediting the Lord's return.

Reformers are not just called to alter their world, but they have the potential to do so through positioning or purely supernatural means. This is not a mere possibility but a promise. God will honor His Word and move with those about His business. The bottom line is this: While we know the written Word of God cannot be broken or altered, and prophecies will be fulfilled, we are not bound by the timelines or natural confines of a world going mad. We have the authority, the calling, and the potential to impact our world significantly.

> **Dear reader,** *if Christ is in you, the hope of glory, you can alter the norms of the time you walk in. God is counting on you and the body of Christ to activate these alterations for His purpose in this generation.*

CHAPTER EIGHT

COME UP HERE!
WATCHMAN CALL TO
A GENERATION

*After these things I looked, and behold, a door standing
open in heaven. And the first voice which I heard was like
a trumpet speaking with me, saying, "Come up here, and
I will show you things which must take place after this."*

—Revelation 4:1

Many are called in their generation by the Voice of God. In my case, they are summoned for a generational and prophetic purpose. Please allow me to share a part of my summoning that released a generational assignment in my life. I desire that you find what God has called you to and that the Spirit of the Living God will summon you to engage with the location, people, and purpose God has for you. That is why I want to share this with you.

I have long believed that the Holy Spirit is summoning many to engage with the *reformation spirit* of Elijah in this generation. One day, the Voice of God found me, like on other occasions, but this time, it was unique, directional, and weighty.

When God speaks, it can be a small voice or through a burning bush. He speaks at different times and in various ways. In the instance that led me to write this book, His Voice was stark and direct. The encounter was supernaturally audible in my intellect and my spirit. The Voice of God came directly at me, knocking me from a standing position into my chair while saying, "Come up here, Joseph! Come up higher, come up where I AM!"

Nothing was unique in my surroundings when this happened. I was standing in a meeting with several other ministers I respected during ministry time. Prophetic ministry was happening at the front of the meeting, and I was simply praying in the Spirit while this took place. As my eyes were fixed on the moment and my heart engaged in prayer over those receiving, that supernatural moment suddenly happened, which I now know impacted me more than I first understood.

While watching that time of ministry, it was as if power opened from the spirit realm and roared across the room like a narrow spotlight in the form of spiritual sound—my eyes and ears were taken over by the Spirit realm with what felt like a flash of lightning. Nothing changed in the natural, but a sudden and spiritually audible snap struck me from the platform of this meeting to the back of the room where I was standing. It was a message for me directly from the throne of God, saying these powerful and highly potent words:

> "Come up here, Joseph, come up higher, come up where I AM!"

These words struck me in my intellect and inner man when they were spoken directly. They caused me to fall into the seat directly behind me. Those words knocked me down! To everyone around me, it was calm and mellow. A simple time of wonderful ministry was taking place in the room. It was an earth-shaking moment that had rocked me from the inside out. Then, as quickly as it came, it was over. All was quiet and normal again.

However, those words stayed with me like a brand on my heart. Experientially, I knew something significant had taken place. I held it in my heart and began to ask the Lord why I heard such a precise word that lines up with Revelation 4:1, which says, "...come up here, and I will show you things which must take place after this."

WAITING ON THE LORD IS NOT A PASSIVE ACTION

I prayed about the words "come up here, come up where I am" for weeks until another moment unfolded. Now, just before telling the next encounter, let me say that it is crucial we don't spend our lives waiting on an encounter or some supernatural experience to do what God tells us to do or as our guide for life. Reading the Bible for a long time is necessary for those seeking the Lord and praying in the Spirit.

GOD IS CALLING MANY INTO ACTION SERVICE

When we seek the Lord or have a supernatural encounter, we should bathe in it by praying in the Spirit and staying firmly in the Word of God throughout the process. Having said this, let me share with you what happened next, as I believe it will shed light on the way God calls many to active duty in this generation.

Once again, by sharing some of my journey, you may discover how God could be calling you to serve actively in response to the spirit of Elijah's arrival in your generation. Answering the specific call that God presents to you is the gateway to engaging the spirit of Elijah and fulfilling your role as a reformer in your generation.

SUMMONED AS A WATCHMAN ON AMERICA'S MOUNTAIN

Only a few weeks after I heard the words, "Come up higher," I found myself praying early one morning, when with great clarity came an inner witness, in the form of an unction or desire, I knew the Holy Spirit was speaking to me. "Get up, go to the top of Pikes Peak," I heard this in my spirit. It was strong on me with a desire to do this, so accompanied by my son Daniel, we got in our pickup truck and started the drive.

Driving up that windy journey was delightful. I prayed in the Spirit the entire way up, and my son agreed. As we approached the summit, we spent some time looking around and identifying other areas surrounding us.

Once we arrived at the summit, we walked around while praying in the Spirit. We found a location to look over the vast landscape before us. Pikes Peak is breathtaking; you can see a tremendous distance into the horizon. While standing high on that summit area, the Spirit of the Lord spoke to me about a prophetic assignment to "America's Mountain." What the Lord was saying began to dawn on me as His Voice grew stronger in me regarding this moment. Going to the zenith of Pikes Peak was a prophetic sign to me.

While standing at the summit of America's mountain, the Lord began to speak to me, saying, "I have called you as a watchman to America." God had summoned and commissioned me to the top of Pikes Peak to get my undivided attention and give me this assignment.

THE PURPLE MOUNTAIN MAJESTY

Some may not know this, but the phrase "purple mountain majesty" in our great national song, "America the Beautiful," is a direct reference to Pikes Peak.

Much of this was the beginning of the fulfillment of a prophetic word my wife and I received many years before that time. The prophecy given to us declared that I would come to a time when our ministry would move to the mountains, and we would become like the mountains around us. This was a representation of ministries and our voice on the earth.

We know this was when the Lord called us to have a specific voice in America, even though we have an international prophetic ministry with a worldwide broadcast. I love all nations and desire to preach the gospel and impact society in every culture—primarily through media!

However, as an international prophetic voice, we have a specific assignment to the United States of America: to call her to repentance, warn her, prepare her, and interpret the signs as the sons of Issachar did in Israel.

COME UP HIGHER BECAME CLEAR

As my son and I stood at the summit area of Pikes Peak, I realized the Holy Spirit was calling me to America as a watchman. I also understood that Pikes Peak is known as America's mountain, and the words "Come up higher" started to become clearer!

Not only was this a revelatory and prophetic watchman calling, but now, standing on America's mountain, I recognized that I was being called as a watchman based in a geographic location representing America. That moment, God reminded me of my studies regarding the apostle John, who, in his later years, wrote 1, 2, and 3 John and finished the book of Revelation in his home overlooking Ephesus.

SENT TO THE SEVEN CHURCHES IN REVELATION

Several months after our divine assignment on the summit of Pikes Peak, my wife, daughter, and I took a trip to Turkey to physically visit the sites of each of the seven churches mentioned in the book of Revelation—a journey led by my dear friend, Rick Renner.

JOHN THE REVELATOR'S HOUSE

While in Ephesus, we had the opportunity to stand on the well-preserved remains of John the Revelator's house. John, who wrote the book of Revelation, was the one who heard the words, "Come up here!" in Revelation 4:1. Standing in that location was a prophetic moment as I heard what John heard, and now I was standing at John's house. God's Voice is so powerful and clear at times. He shows no favoritism, and it was a profound moment to hear those words and find myself standing in the very place where the wonderful man of God lived.

John's house was above the temple of Artemis, where he could hear pagan worship and the sounds of a godless culture. My daughter Ali walked with me as I found a place on the ridge overlooking the temple of Artemis. This scenic overlook was a brief walk away from John's house, and I could imagine John standing there and praying over the temple and city below him.

John was stationed right there! It struck me deeply that God assigns some to a location for His kingdom's purposes. Above that temple on that mountain range, God had John tucked away from the attention of a pagan world gone mad, yet he still made a global impact on the kingdom of God!

While there, my heart was full when I considered John in his later years—an old tenured saint who endured in his generation yet found himself in his later 90s (or older) writing the most incredible piece of inspired prophetic literature in the history of the world! What ministered to me powerfully was realizing John was called to do the assignment God gave him. He was different from all the other apostles, even outliving them by decades.

John was located in one of the ancient world's main epicenters for pagan idolatry, yet thrived in God's will. It was a powerful moment when considering that God not only had a profound calling for John but also, again, has a distinct calling for every person—there is a distinct calling God has for you!

My heart was full while standing at John the Revelator's house, as the Spirit of the Lord was speaking to me and confirming my assignment. I was being called as a watchman to America. In biblical terms, a watchman is appointed by God as a spiritual guardian through prayer to warn of impending danger and to proclaim God's truth. This watchman call rang stronger when I saw where John lived. No matter the climate of the culture, the watchmen are to be situated where God places them as a distribution center of revelation and for understanding the signs of the times.

MARCHING ORDERS

Hearing similar words spoken to John the Revelator in Revelation 4:1 was for a purpose. When it happened, I immediately thanked God for speaking to me and went to that scripture. It was a powerful encounter with an assignment. The words "Come up here, come up higher, come up where I Am" were marching orders! That prophetic song and experience were an invitation to obey the Voice of God.

STANDING ON NOAH'S ARK IN THE MOUNTAINS OF ARARAT

Following these experiences, Heather and I traveled with Rick and Denise Renner, their sons Paul and Joel Renner, and their television crew to the eastern side of Turkey or Armenia in the Mountains of Ararat.

Our destination was to film the site where many believe Noah's Ark is resting. Our first encounter with the ark was very powerful. When we walked toward it in the valley below, as we came around part of the terrain blocking the view of the structure, we entered the space when all obstruction of view was removed, and there was the backside of the ark. We could see the entire object from stern to bow! I looked over at my wife, Heather; her eyes filled with tears. Asking her if she was ok, she replied, "This is where God started over for us. This is where we all began." Her words were perfectly said and summarized precisely the moment we were experiencing.

Our time walking along, filming, and examining the site of Noah's Ark was surreal, yet it was also a prophetic act that the Lord had sent us to accomplish. After the prophetic things the Lord released to us from the moment He said, "Come up here..." We were on a journey that is still going on when this book finds its way to your hands.

This journey led us to what we believe is the resting place of Noah's Ark. While standing there and intently listening to Rick masterfully instruct us on biblical and historical evidence concerning this location, I began receiving the word God wanted me to hear at the Ark location: *America would see a time of instability, but there would be a redemptive plan.*

REDEMPTIVE INSTABILITY

God is calling His reformers to turn the children's hearts to the fathers and the fathers' hearts to the children's. They will do this through days of instability. While standing on the Ark, the word came to me—*redemptive instability*.

The coming generational move of God will be under tremendous times of redemptive instability, much like the narrative of Noah's Ark. Destruction was raging all around, and the world was being flooded and razed to nothing; yet for those on the ark, with a word from God, experienced the ultimate lift above catastrophic judgment.

Those eight passengers lived through the ultimate *redemptive instability*. You are called to do the same. Should Jesus tarry, those who ride above all the instability will experience a time of redemption, restoration, and building for a future generation.

WATCHMAN OF REDEMPTIVE INSTABILITY

By experiencing Noah's Ark, God showed me the purpose these coming reformers will play in their generation. The Holy Spirit is raising watchmen, ministers, believers, and those assigned to accomplish tremendous feats in this generation. All of what these will do will be accomplished in times of great instability, but these reformers are called to bring about redemption in every scenario in which they are anointed to be present.

THE PATH OF REFORMATION

Much of this narrative I'm sharing with you is to unveil the understanding that many are called in this generation to walk the path of reformation. Prophetically, there are times when the Lord uses unique scenarios to shine a light on what He intends to accomplish. I desire for you to walk in the fullness of what the Lord has for you to accomplish—may everyone called to walk their path of obedience find the same in what He has marked them for.

VISION OF A CONCRETE EARTH

Encounters where the Lord spoke to me about what He desired me to do began in the 1990s. In those days, there were powerful worldwide meetings where the power of God was on display. Enormous crowds would gather at specific hotspots of revival, and many came from all around the world to experience these meetings. Two of the most well-known were in Toronto, Canada, and Brownsville, Florida.

Many people were healed, delivered, and saved. I had the privilege of attending the meetings in Brownsville for several days. On the final day of my time there, we boarded the bus home after being in that environment rich in faith and power. While making it to my seat, a profound thing happened to me. It was the beginning of my reformer journey! I was suddenly and supernaturally taken to another place—I was no longer on the bus; everything around me was different.

It wasn't clear to me if I was in or out of my body. What I do know is everything was photo-real. I could empirically observe my surroundings; it seemed corporeal and tangible—no different from any natural setting I've ever stood in. Once my bearings equalized, I began noticing where my feet stood—stony concrete ground but smooth. Everything under my feet was concrete, and all the surrounding terrain was solid concrete. My eyes went up from my feet and looked out in front, and as far as I could see, the buildings and even the trees seemed to be concrete.

THE BREAKER SEED

Sow for yourselves righteousness; reap in mercy; break up your fallow ground, for it is time to seek the Lord, till He comes and rains righteousness on you.

—Hosea 10:12

Everything was concrete! Upon looking down at my right hand, I identified a small white seed in my palm. It was a tiny seed. I didn't determine what kind of seed it was specifically, but I have often referred to it as a mustard seed; however, it was simply a small, white seed. Upon seeing this seed in my right hand, a Voice prompted me to throw it. That little seed violently slammed into the concrete like a multiple-ton wrecking ball had been dropped from 300 feet. Its impact made an explosion, producing a barbaric crunching sound like a meteor strike— it hit the ground with such force that I jumped back in shock!

As the seed punched through that thick concrete, the ground bounced into broken pieces as it sought the soil beneath. The violent breakthrough revealed a large crater with broken concrete slabs standing on end and sideways, the way broken ice would sit if something broke the surface of a frozen lake. Only these concrete remnants were lying in broken pieces inside the slope of this crater, which had a diameter of at least 20 feet. It was astonishing as dirt flew under the broken, thick concrete slab. Suddenly, as that dramatic scene had taken place, a Voice spoke to me, saying, "So shall your words be to the hearts of men!" Those words dramatically altered my heart at that moment. However, the words were sealed up for a future day when the Lord determined. After coming out of the trance or vision, I was still seated on the bus, and Jordan was beside me. To everyone around me, nothing out of the ordinary had happened. I, however, was profoundly impacted by that revelatory moment.[1]

PROPHETIC ACTS

To this day, I don't fully understand prophetic acts and why God chooses to speak through visions and prophetic acts. Still, it has been one mechanism His Holy Spirit has utilized to lead me into the arena of reformation. It is a matter of good housekeeping to always stand firmly on the scripture and never allow an experience to point you away from the Word of God but rather deeper into it. Similar to speaking things out into the natural by prayer, so does standing in a physical location, and more so doing a Holy Spirit-inspired action or spoken word to activate God's desire for a current agenda He is working out. For an in-depth understanding of prophetic encounters and navigating supernatural experiences, please consider reading my book *Demystifying the Prophetic* at JosephZ.com. It will significantly benefit you with a solid biblical foundation regarding all things prophetic.

SPEEDING UP THE TIME

Therefore, since all these things will be dissolved, what manner of persons ought you to be in holy conduct and godliness, [12] **looking for and hastening the coming of the day of God,** *because of which the heavens will be dissolved, being on fire, and the elements will melt with fervent heat?*

—2 Peter 3:11-12

A generational clarion call has now come, awaiting your arrival. It is a mass calling to reformers to rise in the spirit of Elijah! For me, this call was a long journey to a point in time led by the scriptures and daily disciplines of prayer and devouring the Word of God with the occasional prophetic confirmation, even assignment.

There will be different forms, styles, and jurisdictions, yet the same Spirit of God is working through them all. What is vital to recognize in our generation is that a united front is being called into service as reformers push back the spirit of Antichrist assaulting our generation—especially the children!

We understand that reformation is part of the Great Commission. For the Great Commission to reach its highest and best potential, it must be long-lived. As long as any current generation is about the business of God for their time, another time will surely come. First Peter 3:11 states, "It is our holy life that may hasten the return of the Lord." This can be taken in two ways:

1. Jesus will return sooner if we accomplish what He has wanted in every generation.

2. It could be that Jesus may be delayed in returning if the Church is not doing its prescribed assignment. Instead, it is called the great Co-mission, where God and we work together.

Each member of the body of Christ is called to be positioned. Your grace lane is vital to understand. Paul, the apostle, says in Romans 12:3 that by the grace given to him, he could tell his listeners the message he was anointed for. When you find your grace, or what you are marked, called, and set apart for, you are stepping into the role God has for you to bring about the spirit of Elijah.

LAST DAYS ELIJAH INITIATIVE

Behold, I will send you Elijah the prophet before the coming of the great and dreadful day of the Lord: [6] *and he* **shall turn the heart of the fathers to the children, and**

*the heart of the children to their fathers, lest I come and
smite the earth with a curse.*

—Malachi 4:5-6 KJV

I see the wisdom of God in this generation preparing it through
all the navigating and directional positioning to stand in the spirit
of Elijah. It is not a complex issue. It is a clear issue mandated to us
corporately by the Living God. The mandate of Elijah comes alive
generationally when we find our lane! Believers who find their place
in body and their location will be part of the puzzle prepared to be
activated in heaven's Elijah initiative.

*Love has been perfected among us in this: that we may
have boldness in the day of judgment; because as He is, so
are we in this world.*

—1 John 4:17

As He is, so are we in this world, perfectly sums up the Great
Commission. Jesus is working through His Church in this world.
He chooses to work in cooperation with us. He speaks, and we are
to cooperate and act on His will for our generation. Wherever you
are, whatever you do, and whoever you are with, your life can become
activated as part of this last-hour corporate assignment. When God
moves on earth, through His Body, the *Ekklesia*, His will is accomplished on earth as it is in heaven. For the spirit of Elijah to turn the
hearts of the fathers back to the children and the children back to the
fathers requires the body of Christ to walk in alignment.

Know your tribe and where you belong. This even applies if you
cannot move or change locations. You can be effective right where you
are planted. Through prayer, intercession, and, thankfully, technology,
we can all be connected to who we are called to be with, regardless of
where we live. That unification will become effective when God pours

out His purpose and marching orders to rescue the children, save the perishing, preach the gospel, and ultimately rescue a generation by turning their hearts homeward. It takes the body in alignment to see this supernatural mission succeed.

MOMENTS OF PREPARATION

These and other prophetic moments have prepared me for our season and the coming decades. The Lord is calling a generation to prepare for what is coming next generationally. Next, we will see a complete descent into darkness or a lengthened season of mercy on our land. I am convinced that the spirit of Elijah is the answer God is bringing to our generation to rescue and establish God's will in the last days before Jesus' return.

Dear reader, you have a very specific calling and appointed location. The Holy Spirit wants you to hit the mark for your life even more than you do! I pray that a revelatory light will illuminate the eyes of your understanding and direct you to your destiny in Jesus.

CHAPTER NINE

RECONCILIATION OF FATHERS AND CHILDREN

DESTROYING THE CURSE

*I do not write these things to shame you, but as my beloved children I warn you. *[15]* For though you might have ten thousand instructors in Christ, yet you do not have many fathers; for in Christ Jesus I have begotten you through the gospel. *[16]* Therefore I urge you, imitate me.*

—**1 Corinthians 4:14-16**

Fathers are the beginning point of breaking the curse in their place of authority. The spirit of Elijah induces this exchange, where the fathers lead and offer a template for imitation. Having a point of contact and reference means security in sound foundational teaching and, ultimately, a trustworthy place for imitation.

First Corinthians 4:15 mentions "ten thousand instructors." The literal rendering of it means *boy instructors*. Paul is saying that, *though you have ten thousand boy instructors, you do not have many fathers*. He goes on to define what he means. A father is someone you can imitate. Paul urged them to imitate him! He was saying, "Hey! Act like me!" As simple as this may sound, a younger generation needs heroes and leaders to imitate—creating a turning point for those being guided.

NECESSITY OF FATHERS RATHER THAN BOY INSTRUCTORS

Fathers are originators and builders who create something from the ground up. Boy instructors are those who parrot what they have heard. We should all thank God for boy instructors; without them, we would not have widespread teaching and discipleship. However, boy instructors typically hold the reins of an institution during its decline.

This leads to a mutation of the original intent. Examples of healthy legacy happen, yet when a revelation is passed to an upcoming generation, what was once a life-giving word to a generation often becomes institutionalized at the hands of boy instructors. We will discuss this in the chapter "Decline of Institutions."

OPPOSITION TO GENERATIONAL RECONCILIATION

Opposite of God's highest and best is an institutionalized culture within the kingdom of God whose relevance is found in persecuting those with a *"now word"* for their generation. Understanding the words of John the Baptist is the way of real kingdom-minded leaders. "He must increase, but I must decrease" (John 3:30). This statement is at the heart of fathers and mothers in the faith. Originators desire to see what they built outshine them through those who carry on with the message; they are gospel-driven. Legitimate fathers and mothers will seek to establish the next generation in a position to "outshine" what they did! Boy instructors or keepers of an institutionalized revelation will strive to stop the next generation from outshining what they know and deem as the canon of institutional operation.

Discipleship and reaching a lost world through every available means is the legacy they care about first. Not just any discipleship, as all discipleship in the Word of God is powerful and effective, but to avoid the curse and see a generation experience reconciliation, ultimately leading to the curse being averted.

FATHERS AND MOTHERS STRATEGIZE FOR A GENERATION NOT YET BORN!

This will be written for the generation to come, that a people yet to be created may praise the LORD.

—Psalm 102:18

Developed spiritual fathers and mothers will always have the future generation in mind. As they age, they become better at empowering the younger ones in discovering and advancing in whatever field they are called to. When referencing the spirit of Elijah, a generational restoration factor can only occur by God's hand on a cooperating agent. God moves on both an individual and a people. Fathers whose hearts are turned toward the young generation will be at the forefront of visitation or impact from the spirit of Elijah. It starts with the fathers. When fathers do their part, the children will follow.

Every child desires to belong and desperately cries out for a father's approval, guidance, and, most importantly, love. A father's love can shape a child's life, instilling a sense of pride, direction, and security. Love can also guide children through life's challenges and inspire them to reach their full potential.

Few things strip evil of its power like the genuine love and acceptance of a godly father. The union of generations will authorize revelation leading to the re-seizure of designated territory that God ordained since the beginning.

GENERATIONAL EXCHANGE IS THE BEGINNING OF CULTURAL ALTERATIONS

Mercy and truth preserve the king, and by lovingkindness he upholds his throne. ²⁹ *The glory of young men is their strength, and the splendor of old men is their gray head.*

—Proverbs 20:28-29

What do the old have to offer the young? *Wisdom…*

What do the young have to offer the older? *Strength…*

Young ones listening to the elders who are fathering or mothering them is powerful. However, it comes through a supernatural consideration, which takes place when an introduction to the spirit of Elijah is made—breaking the wall of cultural reformation.

How does this take place? Among a culture of hardened hearts, deception, and idolatry comes a reformer, the voice of one crying in the wilderness, shocking the culture and boldly confronting its off-base and misguided wandering. Reformers may come as a bolt of lightning or with a message. These are anointed by God to give a generation the same choice Elijah did by posing the question, "How long will you falter between two opinions?" (1 Kings 18:21).

With this question comes some form of unusual demonstration of the power of God. This may manifest through a special message or other means.

REFORMATION COMBINES WISDOM AND STRENGTH

He will also go before Him in the spirit and power of Elijah, **"to turn the hearts of the fathers to the children,"**

*and the disobedient to the wisdom of the just, to make
ready a people prepared for the Lord.*

—Luke 1:17

It takes a spirit of reformation to turn the hearts of the Fathers to
the children and the children to the fathers. It is also the fathers who
will rise and stop the evil from assaulting the children. If darkness cannot beat fathers, it will attempt to separate them from the children—a
tactic for stopping generational purposes. When there is generational
purpose, there is generational cooperation that causes society to live.
War is won when reconciliation takes place. Mutual respect and cooperation are the result.

*Children's children are the crown of old men, and the
glory of children is their father.*

—Proverbs 17:6

*The glory of young men is their strength, and the splendor
of old men is their gray head.*

—Proverbs 20:29

Darkness hates generational reconciliation because it has the power
to accomplish mighty things. Proverbs 17:6 and Proverbs 20:29 each
point to an aspect of generational cooperation. Children are to be the
crown of old men or in a generational understanding. A healthy generation established by the efforts of a prior generation is most admired
by those who fought and labored to build it. A healthy culture results
when fathers and mothers care and construct a future for those coming after them. Young men possess strength, and old men have gray
hair. Symbolically, what this represents is ability and wisdom working

together. Ability or power is found in the vigor of the young, while wisdom is discovered in the gray hair of the tenured, advanced ones.

It's been said, "Youth is wasted on the young." However, that is not true with generational reconciliation. When the older and younger work together, the by-product is wisdom guiding strength, like the steering of a massive bulldozer. All the power to move large amounts of earth without direction as to where it should be placed leaves a wasted and fruitless experience. A lack of guidance to power is wasteful or even highly destructive. The required leadership, vision, and inspiration are from those who once walked the path and are now available to guide the power of youth along the current path.

THE POWER OF SPIRITUAL FATHERS

When the term "spiritual father" is introduced, it can mean many different things to many people. Some may have a strange idea about what that means. Some utilize the label spiritual father for purposes that are not healthy or biblical. A lot of weirdness has come from phrases or monikers such as *spiritual fathers*. I desire to give you a simple biblical definition of what it appears to be saying. Anything we teach or stand on must have its foundation on the written Word of God.

What is a spiritual father? To answer, let's again look at 1 Corinthians 4:14-16.

FATHERS ARE THOSE YOU CAN IMITATE

I do not write these things to shame you, but as my beloved children I warn you. [15] *For though you might have ten thousand instructors in Christ, yet you do not have many fathers; for in Christ Jesus I have begotten you through the gospel.* [16] *Therefore I urge you, imitate me.*

—1 Corinthians 4:14-16

As we already saw, fathers are originators, but equal to that in importance is the truth that fathers are those you can imitate. Paul said this in verse 16: "Therefore I urge you, imitate me." Paul was instructing his audience to imitate his walk with the Lord.

Returning to the exchange factor of young men's strength and older men's wisdom, we find that when there is an exchange of serving and energy mixed with the guidance of the older man's wisdom, there comes the opportunity for on-the-job learning through observation. Much more is caught than taught when in proximity to a father. Younger people are meant to be fathered but in a biblical way. I believe a spiritual father is typically part of the fivefold ministry. Are there exceptions to that idea? Yes, but generally speaking, the fivefold ministry should be the ones in a station prepared for the edifying and equipping of the saints (Ephesians 4:11-13).

PAUL IDENTIFIED RUFUS' MOTHER AS A MOTHER FOR A TIME IN HIS LIFE

One example of an exception would be Paul's statement in Romans 16:13 (NIV), "Greet Rufus, chosen in the Lord, and his mother, who has been a mother to me, too." Here, Paul makes a comment about Rufus' mother, calling her someone who has been a mother to himself as well.

Here is the main point: to have true generational turning—meaning young and old have their hearts turned to one another—first, is only done by the Spirit of the Lord, and when God implements this action by the Holy Spirit upon a generation, it is labeled the spirit of

Elijah. Because Elijah was generational, he passed along his mantle to Elisha. What a perfect example. Not only did he pass the mantle, representing his standing as a prophet, but per Elisha's request, it was done so with the endowment of the double portion.

Why would Elisha desire a double portion? It was because he was observing and imitating Elijah. When Elisha came to the Jordan, shouting, "Where is the Lord God of Elijah?" He had witnessed the river parting for Elijah; now it was his time, and he acted on what he had observed (2 Kings 2:14). Not only this, but Elisha was to carry out and finish what Elijah had started.

Are there more lessons to be learned from the transfer of mantles and generational turning in the narrative of Elijah and Elisha? Yes, but the main point is that God desires a multiplier with a generational purpose, which is related to young and old working together.

The antithesis of this is found in 1 Kings 13, where we discover a tale of two prophets. The Lord sent a young prophet on an assignment with specific instructions. He was to follow those instructions until his task was finished. However, everything was altered upon the arrival of an older prophet.

> *"For a command came to me by the word of the Lord, 'You shall eat no bread, nor drink water there; do not return by going the way which you came.'"* [18] *He said to him, "I also am a prophet like you, and an angel spoke to me by the word of the Lord, saying, 'Bring him back with you to your house, that he may eat bread and drink water.'" But he lied to him.* [19] *So he went back with him, and ate bread in his house and drank water.* [23] *...It came about after he had eaten bread and after he had drunk, that he saddled the donkey for him, for the prophet whom he had brought back.* [24] *Now when he had gone, a lion met him on the way and killed him, and his body was thrown*

on the road, with the donkey standing beside it; the lion
also was standing beside the body.

—1 Kings 13:17-19, 23-24 NASB1995

When observing 1 Kings 13, the Bible isn't clear why this older prophet lied to the younger. Conjecture can be made as to why this took place, but we know that the older prophet deceived the younger. So often, while walking out the call of God, it takes faith to hear and obey, and sometimes some voices seem as if they would assist, as it can be human nature to believe what someone else heard over what you know God said to you. As was the case with this younger prophet.

The older prophet, among other things, represents a false anointing. It comes to hijack assignments, callings, and destinies. Our young prophet in this story yielded to the lie when he heard, "An angel spoke to me, and you no longer need to obey the Voice of God for yourself. I am a prophet, so follow me." It was a decision that cost the young prophet his life. Such has been the case for many, which may cost them a season, or worse, in this case, it cost the young prophet his life.

Here, we see the representation of the bad influence of the older generation. Old-order institutionalization can act this way toward the *now word* of a reformer. It takes the persuasion of heaven to destroy the curse and merge generations. God's Voice goes out at a time in history, conveying His will, and those who have *ears to hear* from each generation will either respond and obey or ignore it. Those who obey or follow the Voice of God will have an open door to the spirit of Elijah filled with supernatural reconciliation.

Why reconciliation? Because it is the predicated necessity for the entry of a generational purpose. In the time of John the Baptist, he was Elijah, who was to come according to Jesus, but John was also anointed to prepare the way for the Son of God.

The same is true for us today! The spirit of Elijah comes to every generation with the cry of one in the wilderness, saying, "Make straight the way of the Lord!" Or, "Prepare the way of the Lord." Elijah or John the Baptist ushered in Jesus; our generation will do the same through a generational purpose or the actual return of the Lord Jesus Christ.

CHAPTER TEN

THE DECLINE
OF INSTITUTIONS

The institutions of this world are made up of many different systems. Many good and positive institutions offer valuable elements to society. The church and government are institutions. Unfortunately, there are institutions so set in their ways that their former days are so much greater than their future. They stand on the past more than the future, and because of that, when new anointing or what God is trying to do on earth shows up, the old order will often persecute the new. There comes a time when institutions, churches, ministries, or other entities begin to rise, and they go through a growth phase. Through this growth, they get to a high and good position in their mandate and calling. In other words, they hit a high point through growth and excitement.

When that season comes to pass and ends, on the other side of this high point, their entity, calling, or season begins to decline, especially if it's an institution that doesn't have the blessing of the Lord on it. If God had not caused that institution to be what it is, but it had been built on man's efforts, it would have seen a decline. This is a difficult place for an institution because it brings uncertainty about the future and whether it can continue developing. The leader begins to either attack or try to act like a vampire with new things coming along. They try to take hold and feed off the new calls of God. This is evident in places that do not want to raise sons and daughters.

THE INSTITUTION OF THE PHARISEES

…Moses sat to judge the people; and the people stood before Moses from morning until evening. [14] *So when Moses' father-in-law saw all that he did for the people, he said, "What is this thing that you are doing for the people? Why do you alone sit, and the people stand before you from morning until evening?"* [15] *And Moses said to his father-in-law, "Because the people come to me to inquire of God.* [16] *When they have a difficulty, they come to me, and I judge between one and another; and I make known the statutes of God and His laws."* [17] *So Moses' father-in-law said to him, "__The thing that you do is not good.__* [18] *Both you and these people who are with you will surely wear yourselves out. For this thing is too much for you; you are not able to perform it by yourself.* [19] *Listen now to my voice; I will give you counsel, and God will be with you: Stand before God for the people, so that you may bring the difficulties to God.* [20] *And you shall teach them the statutes and the laws, and show them the way in which they must walk and the work they must do.* [21] *Moreover you shall select from all the people able men, such as fear God, men of truth, hating covetousness; and place such over them to be rulers of thousands, rulers of hundreds, rulers of fifties, and rulers of tens.* [22] *And let them judge the people at all times. Then it will be that every great matter they shall bring to you, but every small matter they themselves shall judge. __So it will be easier for you, for they will bear the burden with you.__"*

—Exodus 18:13-22

There is a difference between good and bad institutions. Jesus had interactions with both. Jesus ran into the institution of the Pharisees and Sadducees. The Pharisees were founded on a good foundation. They started because Moses could not govern all the people by himself. His father-in-law came to him and said, "The thing that you do is not good" because Moses was meeting with people from day to evening—meeting, judging, and giving them advice and counsel.

Moses was wearing himself out, meeting with person after person while leading the nation. His father-in-law told him he needed to delegate. Moses listened to Jethro's advice and began to set up a presbytery. He gave authority to several people who could rule with him, and they would help carry the weight of his work in the nation. This was the foundation of the Pharisees.

When you understand where the Pharisaical institution started, you will learn that this is where we get the 70. In the center column reference in the Bible, sometimes you will see LXX referencing the 70 or the Septuagint. This has to do with where the Pharisees came from. The foundation of the Pharisees started with Moses putting the 70 in order, which is why they quoted Moses so often.

JESUS COLLIDED WITH THE INSTITUTION

Over time, the Pharisees let man's rules and ideas get into the pure Word of the Lord. They started on a good foundation but began introducing their ideas and interpretations. The erosion of the truth and intent of God's given institution made the Word of God of no effect. In other words, they began to worship the law rather than the Creator.

They *institutionalized a revelation.* They turned Moses' revelation and systems into a religious institution with rules and regulations that were unbearable and impossible to uphold to the fullest. When Jesus came into the picture and said things against the institution Moses started, the Pharisees became offended.

REFORMERS

So rend your heart, and not your garments; return to the Lord your God, for He is gracious and merciful, slow to anger, and of great kindness; and He relents from doing harm.

—Joel 2:13

Reformers come along and break up the *fallow ground.* They shake the ground to bring a revelation to an institution, returning it to what it was first intended for. Jesus was a reformer and said to the Pharisees, *"Rend your hearts and not your garments. It's time to change and to remember why I called you in the first place."*

This is what God is doing in our generation and with many people. It doesn't matter what age someone is or what tenure they've held. What matters is those who say yes to the Lord. He will rise within and break institutionalism that makes the Word of God of no effect.

There are many reformers throughout the Scripture. John the Baptist was one of them. Many have this notion that being nice people is a Christian principle. Did you know that 500 years ago, the word "nice" did not mean what popular culture has identified it to mean today? In the dictionary, it meant *stupid.* Today, the word "nice" does not mean stupid. However, in the original understanding of it 500 years ago, it meant something very different in the world of the Church and Christianity.

We are to be good people and very gracious and loving to others, but we are not called to lay back and let a wicked society run over our children. Instead, we are to rise and shine and stand up.

THE FUTURE GENERATION

*This will be written for the generation to come, that a
people yet to be created may praise the Lord.*

—Psalm 102:18

God has called you to rise, shine, and stand against wickedness
while walking through this present evil age. Many wonder what will
happen if they stand up for the truth, confront cultural wickedness,
and try to make a pathway for their future generations. Psalm 102:18
references generations to come that will praise the Lord for what we
did during our lifetime in preparation for their arrival. To quote Maximus from *Gladiator*, "What you do in life echoes in eternity." What we
do right now is not just about you, me, or us. It's about our children's
children and posterity. This is why we stand up against wickedness
and evil and begin to push back against institutionalism set in its ways.

Remember that whatever an institution cannot control, it must kill
or persecute. That was the case with John the Baptist, Jesus, and many
others who have stood up throughout history, from the very early days
of Moses to Bonhoeffer.

GIVE UP TO GO UP

*For whoever desires to save his life will lose it, but whoever
loses his life for My sake will find it.*

—Matthew 16:25

Matthew 16:25 means to give up to go up. When we give up to
go up, if we lose our life, we gain it. But those who would try to keep
their life will lose it. Losing our lives means we give up our rights to

shrink back. Hebrews 10:38 says, "Now the just shall live by faith; but if anyone draws back, my soul has no pleasure in him."

If you faint in the day of adversity, your strength is small.
—Proverbs 24:10

Jesus has called you to lose your life, and that means to be selfless, a living sacrifice, and to stand up against institutional malfeasance that wants to choke out the lives of your children's children. How do you do that? You operate in peace that passes understanding.

GENERATIONAL LEADERS

Leaders willing to give up, to go up, to pass the baton, and to celebrate those they pass it to are the lifeblood of generational growth. Corporately and globally, the body of Christ should produce legitimate reformers in each generation.

Healthy reformers taxi the good from the last movement while merging it with the next. These are experts in retrofitting a movement's message and values. I call this breathing life into the institution. It must be stated that reformers are not called to destroy the institution. Instead, they are to breathe life into the institution!

THE INSTITUTIONALIZED CHURCH

For many believers, the institutionalized Church is being confused with the actual Church. I once interviewed George Barna, Director of Research at the Cultural Research Center at Arizona Christian University, and thanked him for his insights into the metrics of ministries and churches. I also asked him questions about his research on the lifespan of institutions within the church world.

Our conversation offered me some interesting takeaways. George's insights show an arc comprising four phases revealing the typical lifespan of a church or ministry.

They are as follows:

1. The *birthing* phase: The infancy.
2. The *growth* phase: The development.
3. The *mature* phase: This group focuses more on its history than its future.
4. The *declining* phase: This group is every ministry's "final frontier."

Institutionalization becomes solidified in number three, the *mature phase*. Institutionalization is what it took to build its platform or position, the unique message preached, and the overall cultural values developed with the doctrinal towers to stand on.

All these things have become a place of familiarity and are good. Yet, they can become the enemy of a ministry's original purpose once it declines.

The decline begins at the point of a fulfilled vision or the end of a movement. It often occurs when the next generation takes over and places extreme value on the principles of what achieved the entity's position. This is what fortifies institutionalism. When a former revelation—now with extreme value that has turned into rules—finds its way to the third generation, it is most often completely institutionalized. There is no more life, nothing new. The past is celebrated more than the future.[1]

WHEN THE HORSE IS DEAD, DISMOUNT

The spirit of Elijah will help you dismount a dead horse.

Several decades ago, a mentor of mine coined a saying, "When the horse is dead...dismount!" This phrase perfectly describes an entity that was once alive and thriving, coming to its conclusion. There are times and seasons for things. Ministries must focus on the gospel and making disciples rather than their legacy and future. It's time to dismount when that horse is dead and incapable of carrying on. There is nothing wrong with that.

A dark side of institutionalized movements can be revealed when they arrive at their decline.

Churches, ministries, or even movements of God that discover they are in decline will begin to understand that their time of influence is over. They often find that their "cutting-edge" days are out of date. As they realize they are no longer relevant, a church or ministry can become violently committed to self-preservation.

The result can be a deformed ministry or organization. If God birthed it, then the blessing of the Lord will keep something going for its designated target. If man birthed it, man will keep it going through every carnal avenue available.

RIGHTSIZING DYING INSTITUTIONS

Human institutions are far deeper ingrained and solidified in society.

Changing these is a matter of what level of institution we are identifying. If it is a sector of business, then it will take voices and special shifts within the business community, showing how they can expand or rightly succeed in the areas they wish to advance in by being shown a better way. In the arena of a nation and the powers who rule it, the circumstances require a higher level of impact. It is interesting to note, however, that business is the engine of democracy, and if you want to impact a democratic society, then the marketplace community must be impacted widely.

I was once invited to pray at a marketplace conference, taking the stage for three minutes, and they asked me to pray and bless the meeting. I intended to do just that. After the first couple minutes, the Holy Spirit began to minister to me about a man sitting in the second row of this event. My attempt to ignore what I sensed about the man was not working. Finally, with the remaining minute or so, I broke my prayer and exhortation and pointed at the man. I was getting a picture of him by the unction of the Holy Spirit. Then I heard the Lord say in my heart, "Tell that man that the universe didn't bring him here. I did!" That is exactly what I shared with this man on the second row. "Sir," I said, "The universe didn't bring you here. God says He did!"

With that, this man was rocked. I said, "You need to get right with God and come here to receive Jesus." As this man leaped from his seat and nearly ran down front to receive Jesus, I realized my time was up. As I was about to leave the stage, a woman shrieked from the back of the room, yelling, "What is happening to me? I have had constant pain in my back for over 35 years, and suddenly, it just went away!" She was sobbing and was making her way to the front.

Next, another person jumped up to repent and receive Jesus. Then, I began seeing in the Spirit about several people in that meeting, and before long, we had a full-throttle revival. The organizers jumped in and participated, which continued until the early morning hours. Business leaders were being impacted, which means they would go back and begin influencing many areas of the culture they were from.

Reformation begins where we stand and take our authority. If we want to impact institutions, we must enter them, which is one of the things the spirit of Elijah does to bring reconciliation.

JESUS GIVES PEACE

*Peace I leave with you, My peace I give to you; not as
the world gives do I give to you. Let not your heart be
troubled, neither let it be afraid.*

—John 14:27

Jesus gives peace that passes all understanding. There's something about people and believers who know who they are and who their God is. When you know who you are and who your God is, you will stand up against every form of wickedness and every demonic influence in the culture. You will shine the gospel's light and push wickedness back to where it came from, the pit of hell. When this is done, it's powerful.

*These things I have spoken to you, that in Me you may
have peace. In the world you will have tribulation; but be
of good cheer, I have overcome the world.*

—John 16:33

"Tribulation" or "trouble" is the Greek word *thlipsis*, and it means *pressure that's so insurmountable that it feels like your very life is being crushed.* Jesus explained that when we feel the culture trying to crush us, pulverize us, destroy our life, "Be of good cheer. I've overcome the world." The word *world* is about the culture, its mood or zeitgeist, and how it views everything. Jesus overcame all of it. We must line up with what He's done to see the fruits and goodness of the Lord in the land of the living.

BOLDNESS

*Love has been perfected among us in this: that we may
have boldness in the day of judgment; because as He is, so*

are we in this world. [18] *There is no fear in love; but perfect love casts out fear, because fear involves torment. But he who fears has not been made perfect in love.* [19] *We love Him because He first loved us.* [20] *If someone says, "I love God," and hates his brother, he is a liar; for he who does not love his brother whom he has seen, how can he love God whom he has not seen?*

—1 John 4:17-20

We can be bold on the Day of Judgment and every day. We should be bold no matter what comes our way, who is in office, or who runs the political landscape. The boldness inside must be manifested and illuminated all around. We are called to overcome this evil age.

The same power that raised Christ Jesus from the dead dwells in you, in your physical body, and it means that in a time of darkness, you can rise, push back against it, and see the goodness of the Lord in the land of the living.

In 1 John 4:17, Jesus talks about the boldness that will stand against a wicked culture and an evil time. The devil runs the systems of this world, and that's why we preach the gospel. The systems of this world need you. They need you to rise and press back against them with truth as a blazing light in the darkness. God wants you to win even more than you do. We must stand up against the darkness because institutions want to choke out the Word of God. They want to crush the life of God out of the believer and bring discouragement or crisis fatigue. We stand up against it by our faith.

STAND IN FAITH

Faith is the power that brings the world to its knees. The word "world" is the Greek word *kosmos*, meaning *the public*. It's the society you're living in and all their norms, values, and ideology they are trying to push upon you. When you rise in faith, it will bring the wicked, Babylonian, dark, institutionalized demon to its knees. Doing this releases a revelation back to a generation. When that begins to happen, you're starting to radiate that *greater is He who is in you than he that is in the world* (1 John 4:4). Consequently, *he that is in the world* is talking about the Antichrist. The Antichrist is not standing among us today, but the spirit of Antichrist is here, and we are pushing that back and making a way where there seems to be no way. We overcome the Antichrist by the blood of the Lamb. This is going red—applying the blood of the Lamb to our lives!

> *And they overcame him by the blood of the Lamb and by the word of their testimony, and they did not love their lives to the death.*
>
> **—Revelation 12:11**

Institutions will become institutionalized when they take hold of a revelation, crystallize it, memorialize it, and put it on the trophy wall. They build a whole scenario around a revelation that was once a living thing, and now, it's like a photo on the wall. God wants to teach us not to institutionalize a revelation but to move so close to the Spirit that we begin to get a revelation to stand against institutional malfeasance that wants to snuff out the Word of God.

We can breathe life even into the institutions that once had a great revelation but have grown stagnant and say the past was better than today and better than the future. We must obey the Lord and stand up in a revelation to bring reformation and a brand-new future. God has something so great for you. Jesus loves you, and there's nothing you can do about it. You might as well surrender to Him. In every way, *Greater is He who is in you than he that is in the world*. Jesus wants your children. He wants them to have a bright future, and that's why we are here.

CHAPTER ELEVEN

BEAST PROOF
REFORMERS AGAINST A
BABYLONIAN SYSTEM

*And I also say to you that you are Peter, and on this rock
I will build My church, and the gates of Hades shall not
prevail against it.*

—Matthew 16:18

A Babylonian system has been in play ever since the Tower of Babel. Left unchecked, they may dominate the land for generations. What a Babylonian system cannot handle is to be opposed by bold, righteous ones who are filled with indignation against the godless society Babylon produces.

The name Babylon is mentioned 300 times in the Bible and represents a society that was against the things and people of God. Let's go back to Nimrod, whose name means *we rebel*, and who ruled Babylon and was the instigator of the fabled Tower of Babel, as described in Genesis 11. Nimrod was the first representation of the Antichrist, and he became a mighty hunter. According to extra-biblical texts, Nimrod was involved in the building of the Tower of Babel. In a sense, Nimrod was attempting to replace Adam, the original son of God. Some consider Nimrod to be the first world ruler, a perversion of what Adam was assigned to do.

The Babylonian System, by definition, is man's way over God's way. It is a pagan system filled with idolatry and self-provision. It states, "We don't need you, God; we rebel and want to handle our destiny without Your interference." It was those who built the Tower of Babel who said, "Let us make a name for ourselves." Again, this is the foundation of a Babylonian system—self is god, self is the provision, and mammon or the love of money is the currency.

THE ANTI-ADAM

He was a mighty hunter before the LORD; therefore it is said, "Like Nimrod the mighty hunter before the LORD."

—Genesis 10:9

[Nimrod] said he would be revenged on God, if he should have a mind to drown the world again; for that he would build a tower too high for the waters to reach. And that he would avenge himself on God for destroying their forefathers.

—Antiquities of the Jews, Book 1, Chapter 4

As previously stated, some say Nimrod was responsible for leading the charge in building the Tower of Babel. According to Josephus, the motivation for building the Tower of Babel was to protect humanity from another flood. Further, according to Josephus, Nimrod "persuaded [his subjects] not to ascribe [their strength] to God, as if it were through his means they were happy, but to believe that it was their own courage which procured that happiness"[1]

If what Josephus suggested about Nimrod was the case, then Nimrod could be classified as a godless, humanistic anti-Adam. Adam, an original son of God who was to rule the garden and subdue the earth, was also referred to in the Bible as *the first man, or Adam.* Jesus is the last Adam (1 Corinthians 15:45).

By referring to Nimrod as the anti-Adam, I am saying he carried the original spirit of Antichrist and raised himself to pervert the purpose of God on the earth through rebellion. Rebellion against God is one of the primary purposes of the Antichrist.

Ever since the fall of man, there have been many false religions and ungodly belief systems attempt to usurp the God of heaven and do things how they wish rather than serve and surrender to the Creator. Much of this is due to the nefarious activities of those mutinous fallen angels who acted according to their will rather than in alignment with God's will. That same spirit has flooded the earth, and we face it today—the *spirit of Antichrist.*

THE ANTICHRIST AND THE BEAST WILL APPEAR ON THE WORLD STAGE

Let no one deceive you by any means; for that Day will not come unless the falling away comes first, and the man of sin is revealed, the son of perdition.

—2 Thessalonians 2:3

All world events lead to the appearance of the one who will come as the imposter to the Messiah. He will initially have answers but will turn against all world religions and name himself higher than all that is called God. That day will come when the man of sin suddenly appears on the world stage; in all the aspects of who and what he will represent, we, the redeemed, stand in the way of his nefarious reign on earth.

In the meantime, we are dealing with the spirit of Antichrist, and the reason it is only in spirit is that the man of sin cannot manifest until the one who restrains (the Church) is taken out of the way. Even though this is so, the Antichrist will eventually rise, and along the way, those who stand up to the spirit of Antichrist and take back the culture will also rise. Such is the story of the Maccabees.

MACCABEES

As stated, history is filled with oppressors met by those who would not back down. In the case of the Maccabees, there is a major type and prophetic instance of an attempted abomination within the temple, which the Antichrist will do again when the actual man of sin appears.

Historically, the spirit of Antichrist attempts to manifest and seize the culture at nearly every available point in society. Here is an example of the spirit of Antichrist attempting to assert dominance over the Jewish people during that intertestamental time frame. A powerful lesson in this instance is what happens when people stand up to the nonsense being forced upon them.

The Apocrypha and Josephus' writings lay out the historical narrative of the Maccabees, who stood up to their Greek/Syrian oppressors in what is known as the Maccabean Revolt, a Jewish rebellion during the years 167–160 BC.

This rebellion rejected Hellenistic/Greek culture. Originating with Alexander the Great, it eventually led to the Hellenization of the modern world. After Alexander's death, the kingdom was separated, and through various wars, the Seleucid Empire won control of the area, impacting the Jews. The Seleucid ideology was the same Greek-speaking agenda that Alexander had started. The Seleucid Empire implemented and enforced the suppression of Jewish worship and religious practice.

WORSHIP OF ZEUS

In 175 BC, Seleucid ruler Antiochus IV came to power, outlawing Jewish religious practices and ordering the worship of the Greek god Zeus. It was a vile act and monumentally offensive to the Jewish people. This oppression led to conflict upon the demand by Antiochus via his officers that the Jews sacrifice a pig to Zeus in the temple in Jerusalem in 167 BC.

The Jews present would not take it anymore and lashed back at the overreach of the Greeks. Mattathias, a Jewish priest, started the rebellion by preventing a Jew from sacrificing a pig to a pagan god, and subsequently, Mattathias killed an officer sent from Antiochus IV.

FATHERS AND SONS SAVED JEWISH CULTURE

Mattathias led the organized resistance along with his five sons: John Gaddi, Simon Thassi, Eleazar Avaran, Jonathan Apphus, and Judas Maccabeus (*Maccabeus* comes from the Hebrew word for "hammer").

After the bloody altercation, Mattathias escaped with his family to the wilderness and hills. From there, they operated in guerilla warfare against the Seleucids and against fellow Jews who compromised by taking on Greek culture. Upon Mattathias' death in 166 BC, his son Judas Maccabeus took command of the rebellion. Judas saw himself as a leader like Moses, Joshua, and Gideon. He was known as Judas "the Hammer" Maccabees.

HANUKKAH

Under Judas' leadership, the Maccabees ultimately captured Jerusalem and rededicated the temple in 164 BC. Hanukkah comes from this event. From there, Maccabeus went to war to reclaim all Jewish territory. In 164 BC, Antiochus IV, or Antiochus Epiphanies, died, and his son, who ruled in his place, allowed the resumption of Jewish practices; however, the war resumed shortly after that, and Judas sought and received help from the fledgling power of Rome to finally throw off Seleucid control. Judas died in about 161 BC and was succeeded by his brother Jonathan. Finally, under Jonathan's leadership, peace was made with Alexander Balas, the Seleucid king, in about 153 BC. After Jonathan, his brother Simon ruled over a semi-independent Jewish nation. With the collapse of the Seleucid Empire in 116 BC, Israel enjoyed full independence until 63 BC.[2]

MACCABEAN REVOLT, A TYPE OF THE SPIRIT OF ELIJAH

This might sound strong, but it could be said that the Maccabean revolt moved in the spirit of Elijah. That is, they stood against the oppression of an evil regime while operating in generational cooperation to see the will of God and His people come to pass in a multigenerational capacity.[3]

NORMALCY BIAS

Our fight is similar to many in generations past; they struggle with normalcy bias. A basic definition of normalcy bias is a cognitive bias that leads people to disbelieve or minimize threat warnings. It causes individuals to underestimate the likelihood of a disaster, when it might affect them, and its potential adverse effects. For example, normalcy bias causes many people to prepare inadequately for natural disasters, stock market crashes, and calamities caused by human error.

Normalcy bias is a passive approach due to cultural conditioning to avoid the issues and avoid dealing with anything uncomfortable, which results in a drift away from cause and the will to act.

Most people know the famous quote most often attributed to Edmond Burke.

> *"The only thing necessary for the triumph*
> *of evil is that good men do nothing...."*

Interestingly, about 80 percent of people reportedly display normalcy bias during a disaster. The answer to such an issue is training. This is why the military has basic training for soldiers to hold their ground and know what to do during a crisis. We, as believers, should do the same. Hebrews 5:14 says *we should exercise our senses to discern between good and evil.* A disciplined Bible reading and meditating lifestyle will break much of the normalcy bias in anyone's life.[4]

JEZEBEL IS FALLEN

Now when Jehu had come to Jezreel, Jezebel heard of it; and she put paint on her eyes and adorned her head, and looked through a window. [31] *Then, as Jehu entered at the gate, she said, "Is it peace, Zimri, murderer of your master?"* [32] *And he looked up at the window, and said, "Who is on my side? Who?" So two or three eunuchs looked out at him.* [33] *Then he said, "Throw her down." So they threw her down, and some of her blood spattered on the wall and on the horses; and he trampled her underfoot.* [34] *And when he had gone in, he ate and drank. Then he said, "Go now, see to this accursed woman, and bury her, for she was a king's daughter." ³⁵ So they went to bury her, but they found no more of her than the skull and the feet and the palms of her hands. ³⁶ Therefore they came back and told him. And he said, "This is the word of the LORD, which He spoke by His servant Elijah the Tishbite, saying, 'On the plot of ground at Jezreel dogs shall eat the flesh of Jezebel; ³⁷ and the corpse of Jezebel shall be as refuse on the surface of the field, in the plot at Jezreel, so that they shall not say, "Here lies Jezebel."'"*

—2 Kings 9:30-37

There comes a point in every evil regime when their day of reckoning transpires. Concerning all the malfeasance and anti-God behavior initiated by Jezebel—her harvest had finally arrived. For in every generation, the spirit of Antichrist takes the opportunity afforded to it, to dominate the culture until the opposing force of light rises to meet it. What is necessary for those who are keepers of the truth, those who are carriers of the light of God in their time—is not to faint but rather stay strong and encouraged while resisting the powers of hell.

Elijah did this until his mantle was transferred to Elisha. Next to Elisha was Jehu, a strong, brazen-faced man whom God raised as part of a correction to the nation. He was an agent of rightsizing the wrongs.

It was due time for Jezebel's destruction. She painted her eyes and adorned her head as she looked through the window. She made her accusatory statement, and Jehu responded, "Who is on my side?" This was a call from Jehu stating that there was about to be a new sheriff in town, and his shout suggested it would be wise to cooperate. The two or three eunuchs heard Jehu and acted accordingly, launching Jezebel out of the window. Her body exploded on the ground, spattering her blood against the wall.

Jehu then had lunch before thinking, "Well, we should go bury the accursed witch." It was too late for that; she had been eaten by dogs.

If the righteous will not faint and not retreat, there comes a day of justice against those who hate God and work diligently to destroy His people. Nothing is more accurate when considering the ultimate end-time enemies. The Antichrist, who will be a man, is likely possessed by Satan himself. In a perversion of the incarnation, a cheap attempt to copy Jesus, the God-man, will emerge. In the end, the beast, his false prophet, and every power who has stood against the Son of the One True Living God will be cast down and defeated, like Jezebel, only in a far more dramatic and violent way.

Remember, in the end, Jesus wins, and so do those who are His.

THE BEAST

Then I stood on the sand of the sea. And I saw a beast rising up out of the sea, having seven heads and ten horns, and on his horns ten crowns, and on his heads a blasphemous name.

—**Revelation 13:1**

Most scholars believe that another name for the Antichrist is the beast. This beast will have a system, but the spirit of Jesus, working through His Church, is anointed to stop the spirit of Antichrist from taking over. The Church acts as a restraining force. The actual Antichrist cannot simply rise at will.

There will be a second beast, which will rise out of the sea. Generations of ink have been spilled, penning vantage points as to exactly who and what this beast is. What can be said with certainty is that this beast appears to be mimicking a resurrection. The second beast gives life to the first beast.

BEAST SYSTEM

He causes all, both small and great, rich and poor, free and slave, to receive a mark on their right hand or on their foreheads, [17] and that no one may buy or sell except one who has the mark or the name of the beast, or the number of his name.

—Revelation 13:16-17

THE CHURCH IS BEAST PROOF

The restrainer must be taken out of the way before the beast can take the world stage.

And now you know what is restraining, that he may be revealed in his own time. [7] For the mystery of lawlessness is already at work; only He who now restrains will do so until He is taken out of the way.

—2 Thessalonians 2:6-7

We who stand firm in the Lord Jesus and bind ourselves to Him and His will being accomplished on earth are part of the *Ekklesia* and are "beast proof." When considering the power of the *Ekklesia* that Jesus explained to Peter, it becomes clear that the system of hell and the complete governmental power of the literal Antichrist cannot appear until the force of the *Ekklesia* is removed. In better terms, the Antichrist is being held back from appearing until the Church is removed. We are the restraining force against his revealing.

THE EKKLESIA CANNOT BE OVERCOME

And I also say to you that you are Peter, and on this rock I will build My church, and the gates of Hades shall not prevail against it.

—**Matthew 16:18**

That dispensation will be different from our current one. We are in the Church Age, and Jesus declared in Matthew 16:18 that *"the gates of hell shall not prevail"* against His Church. Many speculate that this is because the Church of Jesus Christ will be caught up in meeting the Lord in the air before this dreadful time.

For the Lord Himself will descend from heaven with a shout, with the voice of an archangel, and with the trumpet of God. And the dead in Christ will rise first. [17] Then we who are alive and remain shall be caught up together with them in the clouds to meet the Lord in the air. And thus we shall always be with the Lord.

—**1 Thessalonians 4:16-17**

The Greek word *harpazo* is translated as rapiemur, the proper tense of *rapio*, the root of our English words "rapt" and "rapture." *Deinde nos qui vivimus qui relinquimur simul rapiemur cum illis in nubibus obviam Domino in aera et sic semper cum Domino erimus.* 1 Thessalonians 4:17 (Latin Vulgate) "Rapture" comes from the past participle of the verb *rapia*.

One cannot deny that the word appears in the appropriate tense as literally "rapture" in the Latin Vulgate.[5]

The gates of hell cannot overcome us unless we permit it or lay down, not enforcing our authority.

In this dispensation of grace, also known as the Church Age, we, the corporate body of Christ, can stop the gates of hell—a distinction in the Church during the Age of Grace, which means the time of the New Testament.

Shortly following the resurrection of Jesus, a tremendous encounter took place. Acts 2 describes the divine occasion when the Holy Spirit was poured out in power upon all gathered in the upper room. Not only did the baptism in the Holy Spirit occur, causing the believers to speak in different tongues, but it was the arrival of a new power with new authority. The Church, now born during this event, kicked off the last days and arrived to enforce something that had never been seen before. A united group of people were given the authority of God to enforce what Jesus accomplished.

New terminology was used, such as "believers," "brothers and sisters," and "baptism in the Holy Spirit," even the terminology "the Church" was brand-new during that time, and never had anyone been empowered by the Holy Spirit in this manner. God came and dwelt among men through Jesus and took it a step further by making a way for man to become that habitation of God. Anyone who called on the name of Jesus could be saved! Powerfully united against the present evil age, these brand-new species of believers, filled with God, became a global power to be reckoned with.

...These who have turned the world upside down....

—Acts 17:6

THE EKKLESIA

Ekklesia was a governmental word used in ancient history, meaning *the called-out people or assembled body of free citizens in the public affairs of a free state.*

The *ekklesia* was summoned by a "herald" or "messenger" with public authority to represent the kingdom they served. A clearer picture would be the local church coming together at the summons of a preacher.

A broader definition of the *Ekklesia* reaches beyond the local church and includes the global body of believers. The Greek defines it as "those who anywhere, in a city or village, constitute a company, and are united into one body, making up the whole body of Christians scattered throughout the earth." This is a working picture of the Church, both locally and globally.

Understanding the *Ekklesia* (the Church) that Jesus told Peter about makes it clear that it is a powerful entity that He built! Hell, with all its systems and evil, cannot withstand the actual Church!

How is it then that we do not see more victory and taking of territory? Allow me to present you with a thought. What many label the Church today might, in fact, not be the Church, at least not the Church Jesus described. What many well-intending believers have labeled their church as might, in reality, be an institutionalized version of an effectual church impacting the culture.

"Church" was a new moniker. The Old Testament never mentioned it; you might say it was concealed. Many thought the Messiah would come and deliver Israel from all the outside governmental oppression. Groups such as the zealots pressured Jesus to "storm the castle," so to speak, yet He explained the purpose of His coming was not for that. It was to seek and save that which was lost. In His second advent, He will come and take over the world. First, He arrived as the Lamb of God who takes away the sin of the world. His second coming will reveal Him as the Lion, as King Jesus.

"Grace" is the label given to the age we live in. It is a unique moment in history when the gospel is to be preached to the ends of the earth, and then the end will come (Matthew 24).

Jesus referred to the body of believers as "His Church," "and the gates of hell would not prevail against it." The word "church" here is the Greek word *ekklesia*.

BEAST GIVEN POWER TO OVERCOME THE SAINTS

And it was given unto him to make war with the saints, and to overcome them: and power was given him over all kindreds, and tongues, and nations.

—Revelation 13:7 KJV

Revelation 13:7 describes an end-times scenario in which the Antichrist will rule on earth. He will also be granted the ability to make war with the saints and overcome them.

TRIBULATION SAINTS

Those who remain will still be able to discover the truth of Jesus. Some will give their lives to Him, becoming end-time saints. Today's believers will not experience the tribulation. This is why the Word says in 2 Corinthians 6:2, "…Behold, now is the accepted time; behold, now is the day of salvation." Jesus made a way so that no one has to experience the tribulation and all that comes during that time. It's our goal and commission to bring as many of God's lost creations to Him so they don't have to go through the tribulation.

POWER OVER THE NATIONS

And he who overcomes, and keeps My works until the end, to him I will give power over the nations.

—**Revelation 2:26**

One day, I spoke with a dear friend, Pastor Mark Cowart. We were discussing the issue of Jezebel in the Church and holding control over high areas of leadership around the world. Pastor Mark said something that rang like a bell in my spirit. "You know, the church of Thyatira was told that whoever overcomes Jezebel and all her workings would gain power over the nations." This is what Revelation 2:26 means. I had read that scripture many times, but it was illuminated in Pastor Mark's statement.

It is true! As the Church of Jesus, and if we are going to seize the day in our generation, Jezebel, along with all the corrupt issues surrounding that demon, must be overcome, and through it, those who overcome are to keep the works of Jesus until the end.

For every believer who has ears to hear, gaining power over the nations is attained through this understanding. Defeat Jezebel, overcome and keep His works until the end.

OCCUPY UNTIL I COME

*And he called his ten servants, and delivered them ten pounds, and said unto them, **Occupy till I come.***

—**Luke 19:13 KJV**

*So he called ten of his servants, delivered to them ten minas, and said to them, "**Do business till I come.**"*

—Luke 19:13

The word "occupy" here means not merely to "possess," as it often does in our language, but to "improve," to employ "in business," for the purpose of increasing it or of making "profit" on it. The direction was to use this money to gain "more" against his return. So Jesus commands His disciples to "improve" their talents, to make the most of them, to increase their capability of doing good, and to do it "until" He comes to call us hence, by death, to meet Him.

Ultimately, occupation happens through generational cooperation through posterity. When the hearts of the fathers are turned to the children, and vice versa, a curse on the land is avoided. It might be shocking to recognize that certain generations can become so hard-hearted, enamored with sin, and entangled in this world—the only way out is for the reformers to rise. Enter the spirit of Elijah!

ALL THINGS ARE YOURS

There is much to embrace when considering the definition of the Church of Jesus Christ and our role within it.

Therefore let no one boast in men. For all things are yours: [22] *Whether Paul or Apollos or Cephas, or the world or life or death, or things present or things to come—all are yours.* [23] *And you are Christ's, and Christ is God's.*

—1 Corinthians 3:21-23

All things are yours. What a tremendous statement! But what is being said here? For certain, the statement *all things are yours* carries the idea that God will cause all things to work together for good to them who love Him, whether they be the world system, life or death, providence now and hereafter, or any other things; Romans 8:28 says, "And we know that all things work together for good to those who love God, to those who are the called according to His purpose."

GOD CREATED THE WORLD WITH JESUS

God causes all things to work together for the good of those who love Him, yet there is more to this as we continue. First, look at the following passage of scriptures extracted from Proverbs 8:22-31. It has been an intriguing passage to me for many years as it offers a glimpse of creation, but even more so, we capture insight into the progression that Father God and the Lord Jesus love us. Pay close attention to the phrase, "His delight is in the sons of men, and He is the delight of God."

> The LORD possessed me at the beginning of His way, before His works of old. [23] I have been established from everlasting, from the beginning, before there was ever an earth. [24] When there were no depths I was brought forth, when there were no fountains abounding with water. [25] Before the mountains were settled, before the hills, I was brought forth; [26] While as yet He had not made the earth or the fields, or the primal dust of the world. [27] When He prepared the heavens, I was there, when He drew a circle on the face of the deep, [28] when He established the clouds above, when He strengthened the fountains of the deep, [29] when He assigned to the sea its limit, so that the waters would not transgress His command, when He marked out the foundations of the earth, [30] then I was beside Him as a

master craftsman; and **I was daily His delight,** *rejoicing always before Him,* [31] *rejoicing in His inhabited world, and* **my delight was with the sons of men.**

—**Proverbs 8:22-31**

Jesus was with God, creating the world; after all, He is the Word God spoke to create the world (John 1:1). Jesus was a master craftsman by operating as the Word of God among creation and development at the very beginning. Suddenly, we are given an elevated point of view as we read this passage, *"...then I was beside Him as a master craftsman; and I was daily His delight, rejoicing always before Him, rejoicing in His inhabited world, and my delight was the sons of men."*

Simply put, Jesus was the delight of the Father, and humanity was the delight of Jesus! Think about that: God delights in the Son, the Son delights in us, and we are to give glory to the Father through Christ Jesus the Son. It is a cycle that originates from God! Romans 11:36 says, "For of Him and through Him and to Him are all things, to whom be glory forever. Amen."

Knowing this sheds more light on the statement "all things are yours," as we were part of Jesus' delight as He assisted God in creating the world. It could be that Jesus created the world because He wanted us to possess it!

The heaven, even the heavens, are the LORD's; but the earth He has given to the children of men.

—**Psalm 115:16**

AT THIS TIME, CREATION IS
GROANING TO BE LIBERATED

Here and now, reformers understand that Jesus, the Word of God, made this world! This world did not originally belong to the kingdom of darkness; instead, this world was purposed for God's family. Creation wants to be taken back by God's family! What a concept! Romans 8:22 states that creation is groaning and waiting for the sons of God to be revealed. Creation desires to be liberated from a few millennia of being held hostage. How violating that a mutinous angel and his band of rebellious followers held creation at sword point for so long, that is, until Jesus came. Even after Jesus came, a portion of creation still awaits Adam's assignment's fulfillment. Today, it is the sons and daughters of God who are to fulfill the desire of God on the earth, and yes, creation itself is longing for the completion of such a work.

> *For the earnest expectation of the **creation eagerly waits for the revealing of the sons of God**. [20] For the creation was subjected to futility, not willingly, but because of Him who subjected it in hope; [21] because the creation itself also will be delivered from the bondage of corruption into the glorious liberty of the children of God. [22] For we know that the whole **creation groans and labors with birth pangs** together until now.*
>
> **—Romans 8:19-22**

We know from the Word of God that the ultimate restoration of creation will not come into its maturity until the Millennium—when the last Adam, Jesus the Messiah, will rule for one thousand years. He will be rightsizing and correcting much during this time. Consider how awesome that time will be! Jesus will set up His earthly headquarters from Jerusalem and, from that location, institute peace on earth and goodwill toward humankind! Earth itself will benefit from this. Even though we know the world will get worse until the final conflict and confrontation, there will indeed be a complete fulfillment of Adam's assignment to planet Earth.

During this age, however, we conflict with forces that must be driven out. Jezebel is emphasized because she is Elijah's primary antagonist.

TODAY YOU ARE EMPOWERED TO ACCOMPLISH THE WORKS OF GOD

In our day and age, the battle is over territory. Physically and spiritually, the territory is contended for, which is why we must be ambassadors for the gospel of the kingdom. Elijah went toe-to-toe with the spirit of Antichrist working in his day. It manifested through Jezebel and Ahab. The spirit of Antichrist empowers any vile spirit that wishes to dominate culture.

There is wonderful news in this time we are living in. Not only are you called to participate in preparing the way for the return of the Messiah, but it is also a responsibility of the spirit of Elijah and what John the Baptist was to do. We, as believers, are those who are preaching and occupying until the Lord's return. It is encouraging that we have been given all authority through Christ Jesus the Lord in this present age. This authority is our shield and our strength, empowering us to face the challenges of this age with confidence and security.

The Antichrist cannot have you, nor can the powers of darkness. Although we will face many trials and persecutions, what we do know is highly potent.

> *You are of God, little children, and have overcome them, because He who is in you is greater than he who is in the world.*
>
> **—1 John 4:4**

Greater is He (Jesus) who is in you than he (the Antichrist or the spirit of Antichrist) that is in the world. We have a dominating force living within us. Wherever we are and whatever we do for the kingdom, Jesus goes with us. King Jesus resides with us in all things in every place. Therefore, it is our assignment to bring His light into every place we go.

You doing your part in this is part of hastening the coming of the Lord. Know this: God wants you to win even more than you do. God desires for you to walk in revelation, knowledge, healing, joy, and peace with complete deliverance while doing good and destroying the works of the devil. That was Jesus' mode of operation, and it is yours. Fear has no place in your life. God wants you to be free of concern and fear even more than you do. He wants to work with you on His Great Commission to see the purpose of His amazing will come to pass on earth as it is in heaven.

Jesus is with you until the very end of this age and well beyond. Any power of darkness or systems of evil that exalt themselves against the knowledge of God in your life is running right into that greater One who lives within you.

To walk in the spirit of Elijah means to find your place in the body of Christ, be faithful and diligent, find out what God wants you to do, and make your plans big! God is the author of peace and increase. If you set your mind and heart on building His kingdom, God will make a way for you in the amazing saga in which He has placed you in this life to participate.

Be bold, be strong, eagerly desire the return of Jesus, but equal to that desire, be sure to occupy and become immersed in accomplishing His will. You will see unbelievable miracles and opportunities to do the impossible, and the desires of your heart come to pass. God wants you to experience the full quality of life He provided you while you do

His will. Be encouraged that your future is so bright you will have to wear sunglasses to look at it.

Jesus is coming soon! Stay busy doing His will and the work set before you. The future is not fatalistic; much of your future depends on what you do today through prayer, action, and working on the plan God has given you. If you are unsure what His plan is, keep listening to our teachings and keep reading your Bible until the Spirit of Almighty God makes things clear. Serve, study, pray, be tough against difficulty, and watch God powerfully use your life.

Let's get this gospel of the kingdom around the world and keep building lives by the Voice of God. In our day and time, we are to exercise the kingdom of God everywhere we go. The powers of darkness are helpless against the blood-bought company of believers exercising their authority and positioning. Our future is glorious, yet we fight here, now, and today for our children's future, as Psalm 102:18 states, "Let this be written for a generation not yet born." Our obedience to honor and walk in all God has for us to build for future generations is practice for reigning in eternity.

It's only forever. Let's do it for our families, the kingdom of God, and our future with Him. It's all for Him.

For Jesus…

NOTES

CHAPTER ONE

1. Chuck Missler, *The Book of Kings, Commentary Handbook* (Cocoa, FL: Koinonia House, Inc., 2003).

2. Ibid.

3. Greg Laurie, "The Impact of One," Harvest.com, January 15, 2013; https://harvest.org/resources/devotion/the-impact-of -one/; accessed November 17, 2024.

CHAPTER TWO

1. Albert Barnes Commentary on 1 Kings 16:31, *IVP Bible Background Commentary* of 1 Kings 16:31. Ethbaal of Sidon.

2. *Expositor's Bible Commentary*, 1 Kings 16; https://www .studylight.org/commentaries/eng/teb/1-kings-16.html; accessed November 8, 2024.

3. Grant Richison, "Revelation 2:20"; *Verse by Verse Commentary*, versebyversecommentary.com/1998/10/27/revelation-220/; accessed November 8, 2024.

4. Rick Renner, Facebook, October 4, 2019; https://www
    .facebook.com/RickRenner/videos/ahab-and-jezebel/
    376865589921428/; accessed November 8, 2024.

5. John Gill Commentary on Nicolas Acts 6:5.

6. *Expositor's Bible Commentary*, 1 Kings 16:11-34, "The Kings
    of Israel from Zimri to Ahab"; https://biblehub.com/
    commentaries/expositors/1_kings/16.htm; accessed November
    8, 2024.

7. Shelley Hales, "Looking for eunuchs: the galli and Attis in
    Roman art," in Shaun Tougher (ed.), *Eunuchs in Antiquity and
    Beyond* (London: The Classical Press of Wales and Duckworth,
    2002), 91.

    Maarten J. Vermaseren, *Cybele and Attis: the myth and the
    cult*, translated by A. M. H. Lemmers, (London: Thames and
    Hudson, 1977),115: "The Day of Blood (dies sanguinis) is the
    name given to the ceremonies on 24 March. On this day the
    priests flagellated themselves until the blood came and with it
    they sprinkled the effigy and the altars in the temple."

    Kirsten Cronn-Mills, *Transgender Lives: Complex Stories,
    Complex Voices* (Minneapolis, MN: Twenty-First Century
    Books, 2014), 39.

    Teresa J. Hornsby, Deryn Guest, *Transgender, Intersex and
    Biblical Interpretation* (Atlanta, GA: SBL Press, 2016), 47.

    Firmicus Maternus. *De Errore Profanarum Religionum* (Section
    4.1-2), translated by C. Forbes.

    Gary Taylor, (2000). *Castration: An Abbreviated History of
    Western Manhood* (New York: Routledge Publishing, 2000).

8. *IVP Bible Background Commentary*, 1 Kings 16:34, rebuilding
    Jericho.

9. *John Gill's Exposition of the Bible.*

CHAPTER THREE

1. https://www.gotquestions.org/Jonah-angry.html; accessed November 8, 2024.

2. Scripture references and Hebrew word from Finis Dake's *Another Time, Another Place, Another Man* (Lawrenceville, GA: Dake Publishing, 1997).

CHAPTER FOUR

1. Jordan Peterson quote from "Jordan Peterson on You Can't Twist the Fabric of REALITY | No One Gets Away with Anything"; https://www.bing.com/ck/a?!&&p=2761407d9b d37cbd98aee972a6bf4d5ecd60a85a2304702cb64fbd8e446ca 15bJmltdHM9MTczMTU0MjQwMA&ptn=3&ver=2&hsh= 4&fclid=02b9718d-482f-6e7c-385c-64ba49986f42&psq=Jorda n+Peterson+on+You+Can%e2%80%99t+Twist+the+Fabric+ of+REALITY+%7c+No+One+Gets+Away+with+Anything &u=a1aHR0cHM6Ly93d3cueW91dHViZS5jb20vd2F0Y2g_ dj1FNHVWWE1acUtFNA&ntb=1; accessed November 14, 2024.

CHAPTER FIVE

1. *IVP Bible Background Commentary* on 2 Kings 2:3-9.

2. John Gill Commentary on 2 Kings 2:15.

3. Finis Dake Commentary on 2 Kings Chapter 2; Albert Barnes Commentary on 2 Kings Chapter 2.

4. Chuck Smith Commentary on Luke 13:31-32.

5. John Gill Commentary on Mark 8:15.

6. Dake Commentary on "foxes." "Foxes live in dens (Mat 8:20; Luk 9:58); are destructive (Psa 63:10; Son 2:15); and are held in contempt (Neh 4:3). They were used by Samson (Jdg 15:4) and are used figuratively of false prophets (Eze 13:4) and of Herod (Luk 13:32). Some of these references perhaps refer to jackals for both animals were plentiful in Palestine. Christ probably had the destructive, selfish, cunning, and contemptible traits of Herod in mind."

CHAPTER SIX

1. John Wesley Commentary on 1 Chronicles 12:32.

2. *The Treasury of Scripture Knowledge.*

3. E.A. Livingstone, *The Concise Oxford Dictionary of the Christian Church* (Oxford Quick Reference) OUP Oxford, 549.

4. Adam Clark Commentary on 1 Chronicles.

5. https://biblehub.com/hebrew/3045.htm. H3045 = AHLB# 1085-L (V).

6. Ibid.

7. Zodhiates Hebrew Word Study *yiśśaśkār*: Issachar; H3485 (Brown-Driver-Briggs); H7939 = AHLB# 2479 (N); Strong's H5375 *nâśâ'*; Strong's H7939 *śâkâr*; Joseph Z, *Demystifying the*

Prophetic (Shippensburg, PA: Harrison House, 2024), 440.

8. Zodhiates Greek Word Study on "hypocrite."

9. Justo L. Gonzalez, *The Story of Christianity* (New York: HarperOne, 2010).

10. Joseph Z, *Breaking Hell's Economy* (Shippensburg, PA: Harrison House. Kindle Edition, 2022), 180-182.

11. Adam Clark Commentary on 1 Kings 16:31.

CHAPTER SEVEN

1. Chuck Missler, *Learn the Bible in 24 Hours* (New York: Thomas Nelson, 1994), 68.

2. John Gill Commentary on Isaiah 38:8.

3. The Jews have a fable that the day King Ahaz died was shortened ten hours, and now lengthened the same at this season, which brought time right again. According to Gussetius, these were not degrees or marks on a sundial, to know the time of day, for this was a later invention, ascribed to Anaximene's, a disciple of Anaximander (c), two hundred years after this; but were steps or stairs built by Ahaz, to go up from the ground to the roof of the house, on the outside of it, and which might consist of twenty steps or more; and on which the sun cast a shadow all hours of the day, "and this declined ten of these steps", which might be at the window of Hezekiah's bedchamber. (d). Footnote: reference (d) Plin. Nat. Hist. l. 2. c. 76. (d) Vid. Comment. Ebr. p. 859. bring again — cause to return (Jos 10:12-14). In 2Ki 20:9, 2Ki 20:11, the choice is stated to have been given to Hezekiah, whether the shadow

should go forward, or go back, ten degrees. Hezekiah replied, "It is a light thing (a less decisive miracle) for the shadow to go down (its usual direction) ten degrees: nay, but let it return backward ten degrees"; so Isaiah cried to Jehovah that it should be so, and it was so (compare Jos 10:12, Jos 10:14). sundial of Ahaz — Herodotus (2.109) states that the sundial and the division of the day into twelve hours, were invented by the Babylonians; from them Ahaz borrowed the invention. He was one, from his connection with Tiglath-pileser, likely to have done so (2Ki 16:7, 2Ki 16:10). FOOTNOTE: Isaiah 38:8 Jamieson-Fauset-Brown Commentary: There is No mention of any instrument for marking time occurs before this dial of Ahaz, 700 b.c. The first mention of the "hour" is made by Daniel at Babylon (Dan 3:6). Isaiah 38:8 Jamieson-Fauset-Brown Commentary. At all events, there is no need for supposing any revolution of the relative positions of the sun and earth, but merely an effect produced on the shadow (2Ki 20:9-11).

4. Joseph Z, *Demystifying the Prophetic*, 69-72.

CHAPTER EIGHT

1. Joseph Z, *Demystifying the Prophetic*, 364-367.

CHAPTER TEN

1. Interview with Joseph Z and George Barna; https://www .youtube.com/live/4s083Q3C5zY?si=xd_ND8DKQIaDp4ty; accessed November 15, 2024.

CHAPTER ELEVEN

1. https://www.gotquestions.org/Nimrod-in-the-Bible.html.

2. "What happened in the Maccabean Revolt?" *Got Questions;* https://www.gotquestions.org/Maccabean-Revolt.html; accessed November 15, 2024.

3. For the entire history of the Maccabean rebellion, see Josephus' *The Jewish Wars* and in the non-canonical books of 1 and 2 Maccabees.

4. Normalcy Bias: Esther Inglis-Arkell, (May 2, 2013). "The frozen calm of normalcy bias." *Gizmodo.* Retrieved 23 May 2017. Cites: Omer, Haim; Alon, Nahman (1994). "The continuity principle: A unified approach to disaster and trauma," *American Journal of Community Psychology.* 22 (2): 273–287. doi:10.1007/BF02506866. PMID 7977181. S2CID 21140114. Iware Matsuda, (1993). "Loss of human lives induced by the Cyclone of 29–30 April, 1991 in Bangladesh," *GeoJournal.* 31 (4): 319–325. doi:10.1007/BF00812781. S2CID 189879939. Horlick-Jones, T.; Amendola, A.; Casale, R. (1995). Natural Risk and Civil Protection. ISBN 9780419199700. Ripley, Amanda (2 May 2005). "How to Get Out Alive" *TIME Magazine,* 165 (18): 58–62. PMID 16128022.

5. Chuck Missler, *The Rapture: Christianity's Most Preposterous Belief* (Cocoa, FL: Koinonia House, 2014), 20-21.

ABOUT JOSEPH Z

Joseph Z is a Bible teacher, author, broadcaster, and international prophetic voice. Before the age of nine, he began encountering the Voice of God through dreams and visions. This resulted in a journey that has led him to dedicate his life to preaching the gospel and teaching the Bible, often followed by prophetic ministry.

For nearly three decades, Joseph planted churches, founded Bible schools, preached stadium events, and held schools of the prophets around the world. Joseph and his wife, Heather, ministered together for 15 years and made the decision in 2012 to start Z Ministries, a media and conference-based ministry. During this time, they traveled the United States, taking along with them a traveling studio team, live broadcasting from a new location several times a week.

A season came when Heather became very ill due to hereditary kidney failure. After three years of dialysis and several miracles, she received a miracle kidney transplant. Joseph and Heather decided to stop everything, they laid everything down and ministered to their family for nearly three years.

In 2017 Joseph had an encounter with the Lord and received the word to "go live every weekday morning"—Monday through Friday. What started with him, Heather, and a small group of viewers, has turned into a large and faithful online broadcast family. Today, his live broadcasts are reaching millions every month with the gospel and current events—which he has labeled "prophetic journalism." He additionally interviews some of the leading voices in the church, government, and the culture.

He and Heather have two adult children who faithfully work alongside them. Joseph's favorite saying when ending letters, books, or written articles is, "For Jesus." As, "For the testimony of Jesus is the spirit of prophecy" (Revelation 19:10).

Joseph spends his time with his family, writing books, broadcasting, and training others in the Word of God.

From

JOSEPH Z

Thriving in God's Supernatural Economy

There's a war being fought over you! The Kingdom of God offers you divine provision while the Kingdom of Hell fights for territory in your life as a crisis looms on the world's horizon.

Will you break free of Hell's economy? International prophet and Bible teacher Joseph Z say it's urgent to break free now as we rapidly plunge into global difficulties involving worldwide market collapse, bank closures, a digital one-world currency, power grids failing, cyber war, medical deception, natural catastrophes, and unprecedented international conflict.

In *Breaking Hell's Economy*, Joseph makes it clear that we're at a destination in history that requires a revelation of God's supernatural economy—your ultimate defense against rising darkness.

Lay hold of this revelation, defy Hell, and live your life knowing you are destined to thrive in the last days!

Purchase your copy wherever books are sold

Joseph and Heather have ministered together for over 20 years; with a passion to see others be all they are called to be. For many years, Joseph & Heather have had the heart to offer life-changing materials and teaching at no cost to the body of Christ. Today, they have made that a reality by offering various media resources and biblical training free of charge. Joseph and Heather currently reside in Colorado Springs, CO with their two children, Alison and Daniel.

Learn more at
www.josephz.com

For Further Information

If you would like prayer or for further information about Joseph Z Ministries, please call our offices at

(719) 257-8050
or visit **josephz.com/contact**

Visit JosephZ.Com for additional materials

Stay Connected by Downloading the Joseph Z App

Search "Joseph Z" in your preferred app store.

Uncensored Truth

LIVE Chat

Prophetic Journalism

Real Time Prophetic Ministry

Interviews with Leading Voices

Video Archives

Equipping Believers to Walk in the Abundant Life

John 10:10b

Connect with us for fresh content and news about forthcoming books from your favorite authors...

Facebook @ HarrisonHousePublishers

Instagram @ HarrisonHousePublishing

www.harrisonhouse.com